# UNEXPECTED DISCOV

## Beauchief Abbey and Other Sermons

J. W. Rogerson

BEAUCHIEF
ABBEY·PRESS

Published by Beauchief Abbey Press.

Copyright © J W Rogerson, 2013

ISBN:   978-0-9576841-1-9

# UNEXPECTED DISCOVERY

# Contents

# Introduction

My friends at Beauchief Abbey have suggested I should publish some more sermons, and the book will become one of the first publications of the Beauchief Abbey Press. This volume thus follows on from my *Nine O'Clock Service and Other Sermons* published in 2002.[1] I have used the opportunity of this present collection to include sermons that were preached both at the Abbey, and elsewhere. Some other sermons preached during this period (between July 1998 and February 2010) have already been published in other forms. My Lent talks and sermons at the Abbey for 2008, entitled 'Perspectives on the Passion', were produced in a booklet for private circulation to members of the Abbey congregation, and it has been suggested that these might be published later, together with other talks. Another series of sermons on the subject of prayer preached in 2010 formed the basis for my book *The Art of Biblical Prayer* (SPCK 2011).

All the sermons in this book were preached without notes or a script, and I am most grateful to Miss Mary Hodge for transcribing and editing the sermons that I managed to record. I am

---

[1] J. W. Rogerson, *Nine O'Clock Service and Other Sermons*, Sheffield: Urban Theology Unit, 2002.

also grateful to the congregation at Beauchief Abbey for giving me the opportunity to preach regularly at the Abbey. I hope the sermons will not only be of service to the members of the Abbey congregation but also to a wider readership.

J. W. Rogerson                                        September 2013

# Walking with God

*He hath shewed thee, O man, what is good; and what doth the LORD require of thee, but to do justly, and to love mercy, and to walk humbly with thy God?*
**Micah 6:8**

ST PETER'S CHURCH, HOPE , DERBYSHIRE
12TH JULY 1998

These last words from our first reading, "To do justly, to love mercy, and to walk humbly with thy God", a mere eight words in Hebrew, though slightly more in English, have been described as the heart and core, not only of prophetic religion, but of the faith of the Old Testament at its best. And I want to start from this core in a few different directions, to explore ways in which these words are so central, not only for understanding the Old Testament view of faith, but with some help for ourselves.

I want to start with the phrase, "walk humbly with thy God". Now, "humbly" may not be the best or right translation, but we will not go into that. It is the idea of *walking* with God that I want to explore. The background is probably the countryside in which the ancient Israelites lived; a hilly countryside, a countryside where there were not roads, but paths and routes, which were determined by the lie of the land. That is easy enough for us here in the Peak District to understand; one of my favourite short walks is from Edale to Castleton, over Hollins Cross, and I am told that this is a very ancient route, determined by the lie of the land and the needs of the communities who lived in those places. So imagine that you are living in the sort of country where knowing the routes will save you from danger, where learning the right paths from the people who know is important, and you begin to get an idea of what is going on in this passage. The Old Testament is talking about religion as a way of walking, and the Hebrew words *derekh* and *ôrach*, which normally mean "path" or "route", also mean "way" when we are talking about the ways of God. When the Psalmist prays:

the words for "ways" and "paths" are the ordinary words for "path" or "route". We have here a very simple and concrete image, and it works itself out in various ways. For example, the whole idea of what it means to repent is cast in these terms in the Old Testament. The Hebrew word is a very simple one, *shuv*, which means "turn" or "return". The image is of people or individuals walking along the wrong path, a path that will lead them astray, a path that will take them into danger; so the prophetic call is, "Turn, turn around, stop going down that path, retrace your steps, and find the proper path!"

There is something else that is fundamental to Old Testament faith, deriving from the idea of walking, and it is this: that walking in a religious sense is not for the Israelites a *lonely* walking. It is walking *with* someone, here and now; walking with God. We must never forget that for the Old Testament writers and believers there was not much idea of an afterlife, of a world to come. It is this life which is the important life, and the glimmers that there may be of a life to come are really very faint in the Old Testament. But there is none of the rather gloomy Victorian idea that this life is a rather horrid thing we pass through, toiling and travailing, in the hope of something better where we might meet God. For Old Testament faith at its best, life here and now is walking with God. The sense of God in the midst of his people, God-with-us, Emmanuel, is fundamental to the Old Testament. In those important and formative stories of the wilderness wanderings, when the

---

[2] Psalm 25.4

Israelites journey from slavery in Egypt to freedom in the Promised Land, going through a country which they do not know, and surrounded by the dangers of the wilderness, the narrative speaks about God going with his people, and guiding them, as a pillar of cloud by day, and a pillar of fire by night.

That is the corporate sense; but when we come to the application of the idea to the individual, the same is true. The Psalms are the great expressions and treasury of what it means for individual Israelites to wrestle with the idea that God is with them, that God walks with them, even if it does not always seem to go easily, or work out well. In Psalm 23, "The LORD is my shepherd", the imagery I am talking about is there in abundance: "He leads me in the right paths" (or you can translate it, "the paths of righteousness", almost the same thing). When it comes to going through a valley, which is dark as death, the psalmist says, "I shall fear no evil, for thou art with me." If we go to the New Testament and the passage from St John's Gospel in which Jesus says, "I am the way, and the truth, and the life," commentators have pointed out that in this verse Jesus is both the path *and* the prize, and that is simply reflecting again the Old Testament background.

But I want to move to the last but one phrase and talk briefly about the words, "love mercy". The word there translated "mercy" is the Hebrew word *hesedh* and it is one of the most fundamental words connected with God in the Old Testament. It is extremely difficult to translate. The versions vary between "mercy", "loving kindness", "steadfast love", "unfailing love" among other renderings. I think that one reason why it is translated as "mercy" here is it is difficult to talk about "loving love". "Loving steadfast love" would not make much sense in

English either. But that is what it is about, and above all it is about the covenant loyalty of God to his people. The word is used almost exclusively of God, and it describes the Hebrew conception of a God who, having chosen his people, will not let that people go. It is God's steadfast, unfailing, ever-reliable love that is being spoken of. Yet that, in itself, may create a problem. There is a kindness that kills. We can be so protective of our children, or of our students, that we cause rebellion - the desire of people to be themselves. Perhaps one does not want to spend all one's time walking with the same person. Sometimes we want to explore by ourselves, to go off on our own paths, or to be silent and on our own. This is one of the paradoxes of the Old Testament: it is about a God who chooses his people, who loves them with an unfailing love, and yet at times they find that so overwhelming they want to go their own way, perhaps because they do not understand that this love of God is meant to be a liberating love, rather than an enslaving love; a love that shapes people in the way that God wants them to be shaped. In fact, the liberating love of God is a love that wants each of us, in our uniqueness and independence, to develop our gifts and talents, and yet to do this while walking with the God whose steadfast love is always there.

When we put these things together, the idea of walking with God, the idea of God's steadfast love, yet a steadfast love which may be misunderstood so that it seems to be an oppressive love from which one wants to break free, we begin to understand what is going on in the whole of this passage from Micah 6. It begins with God's complaint, God saying, "Look at all these things that I have done for you, and yet you have not wanted to walk in my paths." That accusation is brought against the people and the prophet, on behalf of the people, answers in penitence, "Wherewith shall I come before the LORD, and bow myself before the high God?" And then the word comes to him that we have been considering: it is necessary to do justly, and love mercy, and walk humbly with God.

So we need to keep three things in mind: faith as walking with God and depending on God; yet God's walking with us, if we understand it aright, is not a patronising, enslaving love, but a liberating love; and a Gospel of Good News to a perplexed world.

> He hath shewed thee, O man, what is good; and what doth the LORD require of thee, but to do justly, and to love mercy, and to walk humbly with thy God?

# Do we manage better with, or without, God?

*Then I looked on all the works that my hands had wrought, and on the labour that I had laboured to do: and, behold, all was vanity and vexation of spirit, and there was no profit under the sun.*
**Ecclesiastes 2:11**

ST EDMUND'S CHURCH, CASTLETON
TO MARK THE CASTLETON FESTIVAL
29TH AUGUST 1999

Many of you will be familiar with the story of the vicar who, one day, went past a very beautiful garden. Seeing the gardener there, he said, "Isn't it wonderful what God and man can do together?" to which the gardener replied, "You should have seen it when God had it to himself! It didn't look so grand then." Of course, the gardener was right. The garden, even my very modest garden in Sheffield, is a great *human* achievement. I am grateful for the cotoneasters and the mahonias and the jasmines that I have in my garden. None of them are native to Britain and yet they are collected, nurtured, manufactured and bought (in my case just down the road in Bamford!) to enable me to have a garden that gives so much joy and pleasure. Yes, a truly human achievement.

Unfortunately, I have a little questioning voice, and it begins to say to me: *"Is this an achievement of that same human race responsible for* (and here the little voice quotes from a recent United Nations report about conditions in South East Asia) *'land degradation, deforestation, water pollution, loss of biodiversity, degradation of marine and coastal resources, air pollution and acid rain'?"* I have to admit that it *is* the same human race, though I add indignantly that I am not in favour of, or in any way responsible for, land degradation, deforestation, water pollution, loss of biodiversity, degradation of marine and coastal resources, air pollution and acid rain – at least certainly not in South East Asia! But then the little voice comes back to me and says, *"What is the difference between you, imposing your idea of what a garden should be like - what should be in it and what should not be in it - and people in South East Asia doing things with the natural environment in order to support growing populations, people living in towns, the ever-important needs of capital?"*

Now I am a little taken aback by this, I must confess. When I look at my garden I have to admit that I am a great opponent of rosebay willow herb and conduct a never-ending and never-successful attempt to eliminate this weed from my garden along with the slugs and snails that have completely eliminated my hosta, eaten the leaves of my French hollyhocks and my young lobelia, and goodness knows what else. I particularly dislike, also, the greenfly that disfigure my roses - this year they almost entirely ate up my lupins. I have to admit that I would gladly resort to the various proprietary poisons I can obtain from my local hardware shop in order to eliminate these things, in favour of my garden. But the voice asks, *"Are you doing any better or worse than all these horrid things contained in this United Nations report? Land degradation, deforestation, water pollution, loss of biodiversity, degradation of marine and coastal resources, air pollution and acid rain?"* So I then argue back at the little voice in my head, and say, "Look, you're not suggesting that humans shouldn't try to interfere and control nature? Surely, if we did nothing, we would let diphtheria and smallpox and tuberculosis and malaria and cholera sweep through the human population. Surely, all we are doing in developing vaccines and suchlike is just taking the raw material of nature and using that raw material in different combinations in order to wipe out things that are harmful to the human race. So why should I not use a few of these natural things, and apply them to my greenfly and my slugs and my snails?"

Well, the little voice does not answer that question directly. But it puts to me another question: *"Where do you draw the line?"* it says. *"How far can you go in this idea that because humans are so important in the world of nature, then everything has to be done in order to benefit them? Where do you draw the line? Do you use,"* continues the little voice, *"animals in experiments that will benefit human beings?"* And then, very unfairly indeed I think, the little voice goes on to remind me that in the 20th century there have been rather major attempts at *human* engineering, a little along the lines of what I do in my garden. Think of those concepts of the Nazis in the 1930s to produce a purified human race, to get rid of what they saw as human weeds and rubbish – Jews and gypsies and Democrats and Socialists – and how they sought to breed a master race that did not think, and looked orderly and beautiful, rather like so many beautiful plants in some gardens. I think that is a very unfair thing of my little voice to say, because it reminds me of what our first reading was saying, and what is most marvellously expressed in that most marvellous of books, Ecclesiastes, that to be a human being, whatever else it means, means being caught in a web of contradictions.

I am sure there are answers to some of the questions that my little voice has posed, but they are not complete answers, and I have to accept that part of my being human is to be caught in a web of contradictions. And that makes me do two things. First of all, as I go back to my garden, I remind myself that I am a part of nature. The air I breathe, the water I drink and the food I eat all come from nature, and I share this very tiny part of an enormous universe with other creatures. And I ask myself, "Do I have the right to decide that I am going to kill off slugs and snails because they happen to eat up things they like which happen to be in my garden, and spoil my pleasure? Do I have that right?" At least I suppose I can begin to find ways of capturing and removing slugs and snails in a more gentle way. Unfortunately, I still don't know what to do about the greenfly. I know that ladybirds eat greenfly; but whether that is good news for greenfly, I am not sure - certainly nobody told the greenfly in my garden this year that there were any ladybirds around, and certainly nobody told the ladybirds to come. You see, I cannot answer all the questions because, as a human being, I am caught in a net of contradictions. But if I begin to do my gardening in the sense of someone who is sharing, not controlling, the natural world in which I live, perhaps I shall begin to do it with a little bit more respect for life, and also for other human beings.

But a second thing happens. I am reminded of a passage from the Bible from Isaiah 53. It begins by talking about a plant, which, had it been in my garden, would certainly not have lasted very long. The text speaks of someone who grows up like a young plant. This does not mean a young, tender plant, it just means one that remains weedy and never develops

> He shall grow up before him as a tender plant, and as a root out of a dry ground,

- not a very promising plant. Then it goes on to say about the same person

> He hath no form nor comeliness; and when we shall see him, there is no beauty that we should desire him. He is despised and rejected of men... And we hid as it were our faces from him; he was despised, and we esteemed him not.
> (Isaiah 53.3)

That unpromising plant - an ugly, perhaps handicapped and disfigured person - as we discover as we read further on in the passage, is no less a person than the servant of God, the one of whom people say in words familiar to us through Handel's Messiah, if not from the Bible

> Surely he hath borne our griefs, and carried our sorrows... he was wounded for our transgressions, he was bruised for our iniquities: the chastisement of our peace was upon him; and with his stripes we are healed.

I ask myself as I read those words (and I don't know the answer), "I wonder how many weedy, horrid-looking plants have yielded life-giving substances for the human race. I wonder how many ugly, ill, odd people have been geniuses in music and art and literature and service." Of course, I remember that these words have traditionally been taken to refer to our Lord Jesus Christ, at least in his sufferings. The idea that Jesus could have been disfigured or handicapped is not an idea that has caught on particularly in the history of the Christian Church or its art, but when I think of Jesus, I see someone who is got rid of by the human race, precisely because he does not fit into our ideas of the garden of human life. He is someone who is critical of the political and religious rulers of his day, who sides with the outsiders, who gives hope to the marginalised, someone who does not fit in, who threatens the status quo, and above all who tells us that true humanity (as we heard in our Gospel reading) has to do with sacrifice and service - the life that comes from a life gladly and freely offered. Over the generations there have been many people who understood that part of what it means to be human is to be caught in a web of contradictions and they have looked to the mercy, and the loving kindness, and the forgiveness, and the hope that come from God through that unlikely specimen, Jesus Christ, who would not have survived in our conception of the ideal world.

The vicar said, as he went past the beautiful garden, "Isn't it wonderful what God and man can do together?" Perhaps he wasn't talking so much nonsense after all.

# The unexpected discovery of God

*And Jacob awakened out of his sleep, and said, "Surely*
*the* Lord *is in this place, and I knew it not."*
**Genesis 28:16**

GIVEN AT FESTAL EVENSONG IN LEEDS PARISH CHURCH AS PART OF
AN ANGELFEST HELD TO COMMEMORATE THE COMPLETION OF A
SPECIAL WINDOW OVER THE ENTRANCE PORCH, WHICH HAD AS ITS
THEME JACOB'S DREAM AT BETHEL
12TH SEPTEMBER 1999

"Weren't you nervous, preaching in front of the Archbishop?" That question was put to a young man called Hugh Warner, who was Vicar of Bishopsthorpe, the residence of the Archbishop of York, and who found himself preaching regularly to the Archbishop; and this was no ordinary Archbishop but Dr William Temple, the most brilliant thinker, writer, speaker and leader of the Church of England for generations, and whose death in 1944 at the age of 63 was a blow from which the Church has perhaps never recovered. "Weren't you nervous, having to preach in front of Dr Temple?" And the young man replied as follows: "I never even thought of it. I have been preaching in front of God for the last two years."[3]

I have begun with this story for two reasons. First, I offer it as a modern commentary on the key words from our first reading: "Surely the LORD is in this place; and I knew it not… How dreadful is this place!" The kindly parishioner who put that question to Hugh Warner, like most of us, was so taken in by earthly authority, status and achievement, he forgot that in comparison with God these human things are trifles. Why worry about preaching to Dr Temple, when he was having to preach to God? And to be struck by this thought can be quite mind-numbing, and I think we should all hope that whoever sees the new angel window, with its story of Jacob's ladder, climaxing in these words, "Surely the LORD is in this place; and I knew it not," will get this sense of the overwhelming majesty and transcendence of God which is at the heart of that little story from which I began.

---

[3] Nancy le Plastrier Warner: *Hugh Compton Warner: The story of a vocation*. London: SPCK, 1958, p. 103

But the second reason why I use this story is that it helps us to make the important distinction between a true story and the truth of a story. Now the story happens to be true; there *was* somebody called Hugh Warner who was Vicar of Bishopsthorpe from 1932-1938, and if we are to believe the book written by his wife after his death, the conversation with which I began this sermon actually took place. Now the truth of the story, that an Archbishop is a mere trifle in comparison with God, doesn't depend upon the story having been true. I could have made the story up in the way that Jesus made up the story of the Good Samaritan. But the fact that there probably wasn't a Good Samaritan or a man who was beaten up on his way down from Jerusalem to Jericho, doesn't alter the fact that the story has profound truth.

That takes us into Genesis 28, the story of Jacob's ladder, because, like the parables of Jesus, it is a made-up story, and yet one that is at the same time profoundly true. The Jacob of history is hidden from us behind the mists of time, and what has come down to us through the tradition is that Jacob was a crooked, grasping person - a trickster. But when the Hebrew writers fashioned the story of Jacob, they put two things together to give us this story with its profound truth.

The first piece of raw material they took came from the experience you had, and sometimes can still have, if you visit a temple in the Middle East; for going to a temple is a matter of *going up*. If you go today to Jordan, to the ancient city of Jerash[4] and to the Temple of Artemis you can recapture something of the experience that people had in the ancient world of

---

[4] Ancient Gerasa

*going up* when they went to temples. If you start from the main street, the Cardo Maximus, you go up fifteen steps and pass through a triple archway. You are then faced by seven flights of seven stairs that take you up over fifty feet, and at that point you come to a great open-air platform, on which stood the altar for sacrifice and offering. But then there are three more sets of nine steps, taking you up another twenty feet, and at that point you have arrived at the entrance to the temple proper - a great courtyard. And you enter it by going up more steps, and at the back of that courtyard is the great sacred building, and that is entered that by more steps still. And if you make this pilgrimage up all these steps, it's only when you get (at least in the present-day remains) to the great platform on which the open-air altar stands that you begin to get some sense that above you stands the Temple. Only then do you begin to glimpse the tops of the great pillars that were in the most sacred part of the Temple of Artemis. If we imagine those staircases and the priests and worshippers going up and down them, we have a very good idea of the raw material used by the Hebrew writers when fashioning the story about Jacob's dream. The raw material came from the staircases worshippers had to climb, and from the sense of priests and other people going up and down these staircases, establishing the concourse between heaven and earth. But, secondly, the Hebrew writers drew upon their own experience as believers in God and on the experience of Israel as the people of God; and taking these old stories about Jacob the cheat and the trickster, they inserted significant episodes at two points in the story of Jacob. We have just heard the first of them, the story of Jacob's ladder. The second comes later, in Chapter 32 - the mysterious story of Jacob wrestling.

If you read the story of Jacob, you can see what the Hebrew authors have done. Nowhere in the story of Jacob has Jacob had anything to do with God at all until this point in the narrative; and at this point his world is falling to pieces. He's tried one trick too many. He has cheated his brother Esau out of his father's blessing, and now he is running away from Esau in fear of his life. His future has completely gone; his future indeed is a large question mark. At this point, when he is fleeing for his life and has no foreseeable future, he has an encounter with God, where a future is spoken to him:

> I am the LORD God of Abraham thy father... the land whereon thou liest, to thee will I give it... Behold, I am with thee and will keep thee in all places whither thou goest, and will bring thee again into this land; for I will not leave thee, until I have done that which I have spoken to thee of.[5]

Can it really be that God appears to this crooked trickster? And the answer, in the experience of the Hebrew writers and the experience of the people of God, is Yes! Remarkably, God takes on unpromising material such as this! And for the first time in his life Jacob stops thinking about himself and he is suddenly faced with possibilities he had never realised: that the future can begin to open up for him, a future in God's hands and God's ways. Even so, Jacob reacts selfishly. Why not? *We* react selfishly to the moments of transcendence that God gives us. If we want a God at all, we want a God to be there to serve *our* needs, to direct *our* interests. And the response of Jacob, therefore, is only too human: "If God will be with me, then I will do various things." And, yet there is a speck of gold in this selfish reaction of Jacob, and that speck of

---

[5] Genesis 28:13, 15

gold is taken by God and worked on throughout the story. Jacob will go on and will himself be deceived and tricked, and will have to return to the place from which he fled in order to face up to his brother Esau. And, at that point, we have in Genesis 32 a marvellous prayer of Jacob, which precedes the mysterious story of the wrestling, in which Jacob now in all sincerity through what he has learned says, "I am not worthy of the least of all the mercies, and all the truth, which thou hast shewed unto thy servant."[6]

That, of course, takes us a long way away from our story, the story of Jacob's ladder. We could follow Jacob into the New Testament, to the reading we had from St John about the angels of God ascending and descending upon the Son of Man, but that takes us beyond our brief and beyond our time, and we need to come back to Genesis 28. The truth of this story is a truth that has grasped people down the generations, under the Old Covenant and the New Covenant. It is a truth that can grasp us also - that there can come moments when we become aware of the reality and overpowering majesty of God - all human status and things recede into nothingness in comparison, and we say, "Surely the LORD is in this place; and I knew it not." And we suddenly stop thinking about ourselves, and we glimpse for a moment possibilities we had not imagined, and we see God opening a future for us. If our response is a selfish one, there may yet be a speck of gold in our response which God will take and fashion and work out in our lives, so we may find ourselves saying at some point in all wonder to God, "I am not worthy of the least of all the mercies and all the truth which thou hast shewed unto thy servant."

---

[6] Genesis 32:10

May God grant that all of us and all others who see the angel window are reminded of the story of Jacob. God grant that we may be so grasped by the sense of God's reality and presence that we too embark on that pilgrimage which the Hebrew writer describes in the story of Jacob.

# On living in two worlds

*'Art thou he that should come or do we look for another?'*
**Matthew 11:3**

BEAUCHIEF ABBEY
12TH DECEMBER 1999

Three weeks today we shall have entered a new century. Whether we shall have entered a new millennium is something people argue about, and I will not go into it here. For my part, I do not feel that I am standing on the brink of a new age that is about to dawn. I expect things to carry on very much as they have been doing, with a difference being that when I write letters or sign cheques I'll put the date 2000 as opposed to 1999! But it may be that some of you *do* feel that we are on the brink of something new, and if so, I want to encourage you in that feeling, because I want us to try to capture this morning something of the sense of expectancy contained in the Gospel passage I have just read.

Various things happen to us in our lives that give us a sense something new is about to begin. Perhaps it happens when we leave school or when we finish our studies, when we are looking forward to getting married or retiring, or if there is a new baby on the way. But the best way I can think of illustrating the idea of living in two worlds is this: what happens if you apply for a new job? You may find that you begin to live in two worlds. You have to continue in your old job, of course, and yet you're looking forward, hopefully, to a new job. Will you get it? Perhaps you imagine yourself already in this new role, and you begin to live in imagination in two worlds. Perhaps it affects the world that you already live in, the world of your actual work; perhaps your mind is taken from your actual job while you wonder whether the new job will come or what it will be like. It doesn't matter how we think about it, but it is very important to have this sense of living in two worlds, one that is here and now, and one that is just around the corner, one that we may enter any moment. That is certainly the sense that runs through our Gospel passage today (Matthew 11.2–10), and it characterised the thinking, worship and witness of the Early Church.

The sense that something new is about to begin can be understood, alas, in many different ways. In recent years we have read about awful tragedies where powerful leaders of small sects have persuaded their followers to commit suicide because they thought the world was about to end. I have also heard of Christians today who will not take out insurance, because they think the world is soon going to end and therefore insurance is not necessary.

John the Baptist, the last of the great prophets of the Old Covenant, had a particular view of what would happen when the Day of the Lord came. He saw it as a Day of Judgement - a day when everything that resisted God and was proud and haughty would be swept away - where the wicked would get their comeuppance; and I think we can all have a great deal of sympathy with that. We come, in a few days, to the end of what must have been the most horrendous century in human history. In the past hundred years we, as human beings, have killed millions of our fellow human beings and continue to do so. We have wiped out many of the species with which we share our planet, and have almost brought our planet itself to the verge of extinction (sometimes a reason why people fall away from faith is that they say, quite understandably, "If there is a God, why doesn't he *do* something about the evil and wickedness that is so apparent to us day by day?"). So we can sympathise with somebody, like John the Baptist, who comes along and says, "God is going to put a stop to all that!", and John sends a message to Jesus asking a question. John is in prison; probably in a cave, from where he can look up to the hill we know as Machaerus, on the eastern side of the Dead

Sea. It is sometimes called the Eastern Masada - not as spectacular as Masada, but still magnificent – and we can still see today the remains of a great aqueduct that brought the water from nearby hills to the foot of Machaerus. From his prison in that cave, John will have seen the luxury, the debauchery and the scandal continuing in that palace fortress which represented all the evil he hoped that God would sweep away.

The news John heard about Jesus did not suggest that evil was being dealt with; things seemed to be going on as usual. He, John, was in prison and the people in their palace fortress carried on life as usual. And so he sends his message to Jesus, "Are you really the one that we are expecting? Or should I look for someone else?" The answer Jesus gives is not in terms of a head-on collision with the forces of evil, but rather the creation of something quite different, in which those who are the victims of evil are suddenly given hope and liberation: the blind receiving their sight, the lame walking, the deaf hearing, the dead being raised up (a difficult thought for us, but difficult almost as soon as it was written; people for two thousand years have been trying to explain it!), and the poor having good news preached to them. The Kingdom of God as brought near by Jesus does not confront evil head-on; rather it subverts evil through love. And the Kingdom of Jesus is a kingdom that is characterised by the self-sacrifice and love and self-giving of the One who says on the Cross, and keeps on saying, "Father, forgive them, for they know not what they do." And that forgiving love on the Cross continues with the Resurrection and Pentecost, and is the great power in the world to bring transformation and renewal.

Now, when we bring these two things together, the kingdom as John the Baptist imagined it – a head-on confrontation with evil, with the judgement upon it, and the abolition of the rich and the powerful and the wealthy - when we bring that together with the kingdom as proclaimed by Jesus, based on the power of his love, we get something that is desperately important in theology and for the task of the Church and where, so often, the Church has gone wrong. Let me illustrate it in this way. What sort of news could be preached to the poor? It could be done in two ways: on the one hand, Jesus could preach a purely political message, that the powerful were going to be swept away, and that the poor were going to be in the place of the powerful. But the trouble with that message is that it simply fights evil with evil's own weapons; and we have seen far too often during revolutions that the oppressed simply take the place of the oppressors. At the other extreme Jesus could have said that it was all spiritual: the good news to be preached to the poor was that they had got to put up with being poor, because there was another world coming after they died, and if they had been poor here and now, they would be much better off in the after-world.

Both of these are exaggerations, but they have to be held together, and the practical solution which I would suggest goes something like this: there must be a political dimension to the preaching of the Gospel. In the Old Testament, God says time and again that he did not release people from slavery from Egypt so they could enslave each other. Jesus did not come into our world so it could remain an unaltered world, with cruelty and oppression. But what we need to do, bringing together the political and the spiritual, is to say that if as human beings we have any hope of making a better world, we can only do it in humility, we can only do it in the consciousness of our weakness and our unworthiness; and the Church in my opinion needs always to be criticising the politics of confrontation, where each party says, "*We* know what should be done, and anybody who thinks differently is entirely wrong", and after a change of government the new party in government says, "*We* have all the answers, and all the faults come from the people who were there before." This is surely utter nonsense, and yet we have to put up with it. What we need is a politics of compassion, a politics of co-operation, a politics of realizing that there are many sources for the ideas that we need to create a better world.

We need to carry out politics - our attempts to change the world - in humility and prayer and seeking God's forgiveness. In other words, we need to hold together the view of John the Baptist that evil must be abolished head-on, and the kingdom as preached by Jesus, a kingdom of love and mercy, directed towards our weaknesses. But there is one other thing Christians should do, and that is to celebrate the fact that in the world in which we live we have marvellous and gracious anticipations of God's mercy towards us. Nowhere is that better summed up than in one of the greatest gifts the Church of England has ever given to Christianity; the prayer we shall say together in a moment that sums up our reliance, wholly, upon the love and mercy of God:

> We do not presume to come to this thy Table, O merciful Lord, trusting in our own righteousness, but in thy manifold and great mercies. We are not worthy so much as to gather up the crumbs under thy Table. But thou art the same Lord, whose property is always to have mercy.[7]

---

[7] From the Order of the Administration of the Lord's Supper or Holy Communion (Book of Common Prayer)

# What does the Bible say about marriage and human relationships?

*And Jesus looked round about on them which sat about him, and said, Behold my mother and my brethren! For whosoever shall do the will of God, the same is my brother, and my sister, and mother.*

**Mark 3:35**

ST MARK'S CHURCH, BROOMHILL, SHEFFIELD
2ND APRIL 2000

What does the Bible, and therefore Jewish-Christian tradition, say about marriage and relationships? An answer you will commonly find given today is based on Genesis 2:24:

> Therefore shall a man leave his father and his mother, and shall cleave unto his wife: and they be one flesh.

It is often added, on the basis of that passage, that what the Bible teaches and what Judaeo-Christian tradition and practice should uphold is, as one writer has succinctly put it, 'one man, one woman - for keeps.'[8] I don't need to work out the implications of that for many of the problems of sexuality we face today. The trouble is, the Bible proves far too much if you use it that way. If Genesis 2:24 does teach, and I doubt it does, 'one man, one woman - for keeps', it is quite clear that elsewhere, in the Letter to the Ephesians, the Bible teaches that wives should be subordinate to their husbands (Ephesians 5.22). In my Durham days, I used to read with a mixture of amusement and frustration essays by evangelical women who wanted 'one man, one woman - for keeps', but didn't want wives to be subordinate to their husbands! I don't think I was ever convinced by any of them that they had a good reason for preferring the one biblical passage over the other.

I want to go along a quite different track this morning, and talk about parts of the Bible not usually thought of in this connection, to see where they lead us. Now, we have in the Old and New Testaments many stories about families, and

---

[8] M. Green, 'Homosexuality and the Christian – an overview' in M. Green, D. Holloway, D. Watson, *The Church and Homosexuality. A Positive Answer to the Current Debate*, London: Hodder and Stoughton, 1980, p. 27.

sometimes these stories are far from reassuring. Abraham, for example, who has an infertile wife, Sarah, and desperately needs an heir, has intercourse with his wife's maid Hagar, and a son, Ishmael, is born as a result. But as soon as the son has arrived there is tension in the family and the tension becomes worse when Sarah becomes pregnant and has a son, Isaac. Sarah persuades Abraham to drive Hagar and Ishmael out of the household and into the wilderness. In this way, Abraham achieves what we might regard as the proper kind of family: one man, one woman, and a child. Yet I doubt whether any of us would approve of the method of achieving this regular family, involving the driving out into the wilderness of the defenceless maidservant and her son. Indeed, the narrative makes it quite clear that God disapproves of this action. God sends an angel to comfort and succour Hagar and her son after they have been driven out.

If we read the story of Moses, we come across a deep split in that family when Moses marries a black woman and is severely criticised by his sister Miriam and his brother Aaron.[9] That story has a dreadfully modern ring when we think about the attack recently on the male friend of the black British athlete Ashir Hansen. If we go to the family of David, things become even more alarming. David has a number of wives (we must remember that in the Old Testament, society is polygamous and its men legitimately have more than one wife). David's son Amnon rapes his half-sister Tamar, and Tamar's full brother, Absalom, then kills Amnon out of revenge. David looks on, a helpless person, in this awful family saga.[10]

---

[9] Numbers 12:1

[10] 2 Samuel 13:1-39

But we cannot and must not restrict our attention simply to the Old Testament. In a verse a little before today's Gospel passage, we are told that when the family of Jesus heard what he was doing, they went out to seize him, for (as they said in the rather measured language of the Authorised Version) "He is beside himself",[11] or as more modern translators have forcibly put it, "He's gone mad." We have a picture of the family of Jesus saying, on the basis of the actions of Jesus, that he has gone mad! This has been such an unwelcome thought to some translators of the Bible that if you look in your pew Bibles at the RSV of Mark 3:21, you will see the translators have tried to soften it by saying it wasn't the family who said that Jesus had gone mad; it was the general public that said it. However, there can be no doubt it was the family of Jesus that said of him, "He has gone out of his mind", and this is a very different picture from the cosy stained-glass-window idea that we are encouraged to have of the Holy Family, held up to us as a shining example.

What these examples show is that the biblical story is aware of the fact that within families there can be abuse, conflict, alienation. Now it doesn't follow that all families are like that. Thank God families are not like the ones portrayed on Coronation Street, or East Enders or Brookside! And many people here this morning will be able to give thanks for the kind of families in which relationships have been ennobling and fruitful. The point is that the Bible, whatever else it is, is realistic and it recognises what can happen in families. We have to ask ourselves in terms of the Gospel and the practice of the Church whether it is the intention of the Gospel that people

---

[11] Mark 3:21

should become, and remain, trapped in abusive, divisive, confrontational relationships for the whole of their lives, simply for the sake of maintaining the sanctity of a certain type of institution.

The next point is that, being aware that human weaknesses within family structures can bring about abuse, breakdown, and confrontation, the Bible goes out of its way to take emergency action in such cases. We know that in the late seventh century in Judah, family relationships and the things that they were expected to do had broken down to the point where the legislator of the Book of Deuteronomy introduced what we call "the brother ethic" (including women as well as men, of course), saying it was the duty of each Israelite to care for his or her fellow-Israelite in a way that ideally should be done within the family:

> If there be among you a poor man, of one of thy brethren within any of thy gates in thy land which the LORD thy God giveth thee, thou shalt not harden thine heart, nor shut thine hand from thy poor brother; but thou shalt open thine hand wide unto him, and shalt surely lend him sufficient for his need ...thou shalt surely give him, and thine heart shall not be grieved when thou givest unto him ... thou shalt open thine hand wide unto thy brother, to thy poor, and to thy needy, in thy land.[12]

There is another interesting institution in the Book of Deuteronomy. If a man dies childless, it is the duty of his brother to marry the widow and to produce children who will be named after the dead man.[13] And a rather looser version of that law is

---

[12] Deuteronomy 15:7-8, 10-11

[13] Deuteronomy 25:5-10

at the heart of the story of the Book of Ruth, where the child-less Naomi is enabled through the practice of this (from the traditional Christian point of view of marriage) somewhat ir-regular procedure to have a family and to give thanks to God, and for the women at the end of Ruth to say, "A son has been born to Naomi."[14]

Passing to the New Testament, in the Early Church experiments were made with different types of family relationship, without wanting to undermine what we would today call "the nuclear family." But in our Gospel reading today, we have a broadening of the idea of what the terms mother, father, brother and sister may mean within the context of Christian discipleship. And in the second century Church,a very important institution was that of virginity - a vocation which among other things empowered women, giving them freedom from the restrictions and subordination that they would have suffered in the ordinary conventions of marriage in the Graeco-Roman world.

Where does this leave us in our current situation, where 38% of babies are apparently born outside marriage, where 30% of marriages are second marriages, where over 20% of children live in one-parent families and where, apparently, if trends continue, 28% of children under the age of sixteen will have grown up in homes where there was a divorce. It seems to me, taking what one might call biblical principles, the thing that has to be stressed above all is the question of loyalty. God is loyal to us against all the odds. And one of the important things about being human is being loyal to other people, espe-

---

[14] Ruth 4.17

cially those closest to us. Loyalty enables us to rise above the narrow limitations of strict self-interest. We find fulfilment in loyalty to others and in serving others, and betrayal of loyalty can be deeply wounding and disintegrating. People who have been betrayed in loyalty can be destroyed to the point where they may find it difficult ever to trust anyone again. And we have to remember that certainly within the Anglican tradition of the understanding of what marriage is, loyalty has always been stressed in that what constitutes marriage is the consent which two parties give to each other to be together in a relationship. To quote the words of the Book of Common Prayer,

> Forasmuch as N and N have consented together in holy wedlock, and have witnessed the same before God and this company, and thereto have given and pledged their troth either to other, and have declared the same by giving and receiving of a Ring, and by joining of hands; I pronounce that they be Man and Wife together.

But loyalty is a fragile plant, because as human beings we are fragile creatures, and we live in a society where we are bombarded almost daily through newspapers and magazines and other forms of media with examples of infidelity and disloyalty. It is in this atmosphere that we have to think in terms not only of working out loyalty, but listening to what the Gospel says when, because of our human frailties, our loyalties break down. Loyalty cannot be legislated; you cannot make people loyal by law, and yet this fragile plant that we call loyalty can be supported institutionally and legally. This is why the Church has traditionally taught that ideally, marriage is a lifelong union between two partners consenting together. The aim is to try to provide the support for a loyalty which, however, can only come from human commitment and human affection. And a fundamental theological and practical point we have to work out (and we may have to work it out in different ways, depending on who we are and our background) is the extent to which we emphasise the framework that supports the loyalty, at the expense of the fragile human relationships that the framework is supposed to support. How do we proceed when loyalties break down and people are hurt and relationships need to be re-created? The Bible does not give us direct answers to these questions, but there is enough in the Bible to show an awareness of the problems of living in relationship within the community and of the need to take particular steps to deal with particular situations.

As I have been preparing the sermon this week, a verse from the Psalms has kept floating into my mind. In one way perhaps it has nothing to do with what I have been saying and it is in itself rather paradoxical, and yet I want to leave you with this verse from Psalm 130:4. In the version familiar to us from the Book of Common Prayer it reads, speaking to God:

> There is mercy with thee;
> therefore shalt thou be feared

or as we might translate it in a modern idiom:

> With you, O God, there is pardon and forgiveness;
> therefore we hold you in awe and reverence.

# The parable of the wise and foolish virgins

*Then shall the kingdom of heaven be likened unto ten virgins, which took their lamps, and went forth to meet the bridegroom. And five of them were wise, and five were foolish.*
**Matthew 25:1-2**

BEAUCHIEF ABBEY
THIRD SUNDAY BEFORE ADVENT
23RD NOVEMBER 2003

The Parable of the Wise and Foolish Virgins is not the easiest of the parables of Jesus to understand. The wedding ceremonies which form its background are different from the ones we are used to; and at two points we can be forgiven for thinking it is rather unfair. Why wouldn't the wise virgins share some of their oil with the foolish ones? Wasn't it rather selfish of them to keep their oil to themselves? And wasn't it rather unfair at the end that when, having gone to the trouble of purchasing oil, the foolish virgins arrived back at the place where the wedding feast was being held, the door was locked, and they weren't given entry?

Perhaps we can dispose of some, if not all, of those difficulties if we think about the details. In the wedding being spoken of, an important part of the ceremony was when the bridegroom conducted his bride from her father's house to his own house. That marked her change of status from being a daughter to being a wife. The job of the ten maidens was to provide what we call a guard of honour. They were to go out from the bridegroom's house, meet the procession and then, as the bride and bridegroom entered the house, they would stand (I'd imagine) five either side, holding aloft their torches. The word "torch" (rather than the word "lamp" found in the usual translations) is another thing that I have to talk about. We are not to think of lamps as little vessels filled with oil, with a little wick at one end, such as those we sometimes see illustrated. We only have to think about that to realise such a lamp would be blown out in no time in the out-of-doors and, in any case, wouldn't give much light to a procession arriving at midnight. We have to think rather in terms of torches; pieces of wood with a metal reservoir filled with oil, wrapped around with cloths or rags. The oil would soak into the cloths or rags and when lit, would burn for an hour or two. What happens in the story is that the wise virgins have enough oil in their reservoirs to soak into the rags and keep the rags burning. The foolish virgins have only a little oil, and with the delay in the arrival of the bridegroom the rags have dried out. When the foolish maidens light their rags, they initially catch light, but then immediately go out. The rags of the wise maidens, having plenty of oil to keep them moist, burn long enough for the required job. As soon as we realise the type of torches being used, we realise the impossibility of transferring oil from one torch to another. The wise virgins are not being as selfish as it seems when they refuse the request of the foolish virgins for some of their oil.

We progress with the story. The foolish virgins go and try to knock up out of bed some dealer who will sell them oil (no doubt at more than the going rate for having been woken up and inconvenienced in the middle of the night). They then come back to the place where the wedding is being held, and the door is closed. Now this, for me, is the difficult bit, because such occasions were family and village occasions. Anybody could come. There was open house. And so why would the door be closed? And then, again, it seems to be the bridegroom who speaks to the five foolish virgins and he certainly wouldn't have been in charge of the door; it would have been the task of some servant or perhaps the master of ceremonies at the festival. So there is a difficulty. The first hearers and readers of the parable would have realised at this point that it ceases to be a story simply about a wedding, and that it has a deeper meaning. In the understanding of the first members of the Church, the bridegroom is Christ. And therefore although the parable is set within a wedding, it points beyond itself to something deeper; and we have to ask then, what is that something deeper?

Over the years interpreters have tried to identify what the oil might signify. Does it mean faith, or works, or grace? There is, in fact, a much simpler way of understanding the story, without trying to find hidden meanings for the oil. It is simply this. The maidens were there for one purpose and one purpose only - to go and meet and to act as a guard of honour for the bridegroom. Perhaps they were being hired for a small payment for that purpose. That was their job. Everything they were doing needed to be aimed towards that task and fulfilling that function. In the event five didn't make it. If we could imagine ourselves back to the wedding procession for a moment, how pathetic three maidens on one side and two on the other would have looked, compared with the intended five on one side, five on the other!

Now this, I think, is what the parable is saying to the earliest Church and to ourselves. It is a reminder that what we do in life must have one specific aim. As Christians, we are disciples of Jesus Christ, and that is the fact which governs, or should govern, everything we do. It should affect our whole understanding of life. The parable in this way is a timely reminder to us at the end of the Church's Year, before we begin next week with the solemn season of Advent, with its great final themes of death, judgement, hell, heaven. It is a timely reminder that anyone who lives a life lives it in a particular context, with something in view. For some people that may be getting rich; it may be building a reputation, making a name for themselves. There are lots of different things and some of them are quite right and proper, but for Christians the realisation is always there that we are followers of Jesus Christ. As we said a moment ago in the Creed, we look for his coming again in glory to judge the living and the dead, we look for the establishment of his kingdom, a kingdom that will have no end. That, therefore, is the reminder to us of the horizon in terms of which we think about our lives and to which we relate all that we do in our lives.

Coming back to the end of the parable, does this mean that those who fail in this task are not going to enter the kingdom? Will the door be shut on some people, and as they knock they hear the answer, "I do not know you." I don't know the answer to that question, but one thing I am certain of is this: that the One to whose coming again in glory we look is the One who long ago *came*; the One who is to come, is the One who has *already come*. And the reason for his already coming was not to condemn the world, but to save the world; and we remind ourselves that there is a wideness in the mercy of God which is above all that we hope and desire. But at this time of the year, so we do not take that mercy for granted, so that we do not cheapen it, we are reminded in our parable of the cosmic significance of our discipleship: that we are directly and intimately related not just with the child in the manger; we are directly and intimately related with the King of Kings, Lord of Lords, the One who, as we hope, will reign and put evil in subjection under his feet. It is a reminder in that cosmic context that, as Christians, we should always be ready.

# *Angels*

*Behold, I will send my messenger, and he shall prepare the way before me: and the LORD whom ye seek, shall suddenly come to his temple.*
**Malachi 3:1**

ST AUGUSTINE'S CHURCH, ENDCLIFFE, SHEFFIELD
8TH DECEMBER 2003

I have been thinking this week about angels. It all started last weekend, when we took my nine year old nephew to see the Sheffield schools' production of the opera by Humperdinck, *Hansel and Gretel.* If you know that opera, you will remember that the two children, Hansel and Gretel, having not got on very well with their mother, are sent out into the wood to collect strawberries. While there, they lose their way, they don't know how to get back home, night falls and they become very frightened. The Sandman, whose job it is to throw sand in the eyes of children and make them go to sleep, appears. But just before they go to sleep, they say their evening prayer:

> When at night I go to sleep
> Fourteen angels watch do keep:
> Two my head are guarding,
> Two my feet are guiding,
> Two are on my right hand,
> Two are on my left;
> Two who warmly cover,
> Two who o'er me hover,
> Two to whom 'tis given
> To guide my steps to heaven.

And there then follows in the opera one of the most tear-jerking scenes that I know. While the orchestra plays some really beautiful music, fourteen angels come; they surround the boy and the girl, and watch over them until the morning.

Is this a lot of sentimental nonsense? Well, whether we think so or not, we hear a lot about angels in our Christmas readings. If we have not already sung *Hark! the herald angels sing,* we shall be doing so shortly. And that carol is based upon a reading that we are bound to hear at Christmas, about the shepherds abiding in the fields, keeping watch by night over their flocks. An angel of the Lord appears to them, and tells them what is happening in Bethlehem. When he has told them the news, we read,

> Suddenly, there was with the angel a multitude of the heavenly host, praising God and saying, 'Glory to God in the highest.'

Now, it is easy to take this sort of reading for granted and not to think about it or all the angels involved; but what are we to make of it? Do we think it happened exactly as told in the story? That there were the shepherds, that the angel came, and suddenly the shepherds saw the whole heavens filled with the angels? Well, if it did happen like that, one thing is clear – it is not our experience or, at any rate, it is not my experience. I do not regularly see angels, or regularly get told things by angels, or indeed see the angelic host of heaven on full display. And while we might say, well, of course, this was a one-off occasion and it isn't every day that the Son of God is born into the world, there are also many other references in the Bible to angels that fall quite outside our normal experience. And so we might take another tack: we might say that Luke 2 is the kind of writing in which the author tries to show the *meaning* of what happened, and on that first Christmas Day, really nobody knew what was happening and what its significance was. Only much later, when they realised its significance, was this lovely story put together involving shepherds and angels.

Well, that might appeal to you and it might not - but there is something much more important than whether we think the story happened literally, or whatever we may think about angels, and it is this: that the world in which we live in spite of all its imperfections and difficulties is *God's* world. And in

God's world, God is active and God can and does make himself known to men and to women and to children. Many Christians, as they look back over their lives (and I would number myself among them) will point to particular incidents - a chance meeting with someone, or a friendship, a book that was read, a sermon that was heard, a piece of music that was heard - some incident. And looking back on that event, we are moved to say God was particularly at work, "It was a turning point in my life, it brought me into a completely new dimension". And some people might want to say it was an angel involved, others that it was the Holy Spirit of God, others God working directly. And the purpose of this is not to provide us with material for a spiritual ego-trip, so that we can go round boasting to people of what great people we are spiritually. The purpose of it is a reminder that in God's world, God is at work, and part of the process by which we move from God being for us as just an idea, or an hypothesis, to God being the *living* God, is the discovery and recognition that the things that have happened in our lives to alter our lives, can only have been the work of God. This is the important thing about angels. Angels are a testimony, whatever we may think of them, to the fact that in a world where there is so much that seems to be mechanical and electronic, there is also God personally at work in people's lives, and wishing to work in our lives, wishing us to become aware of that fact, so that God moves from being merely an idea to being the living God, to being a living presence.

We had an angel in our first reading, in fact. Malachi begins by saying that God is going to send his messenger, and in Hebrew, the word for "messenger" is the same word as for "angel". Christians, as our Gospel shows, have thought of that messenger in terms of John the Baptist; but there is a strand of

Jewish interpretation that sees in the messenger an angel from heaven. It doesn't matter which it is. The important thing is that we recognise that God is at work in his own world; and in the case of this particular angel or messenger in Malachi, he comes not so much to give support and comfort, as to bring judgement. And in the reading that judgement begins with the sons of Levi, and that means (within the context of the Old Testament) the Temple and its priesthood and its servants. And in the case of the Church, it means ourselves and the ministers and the priests. And that is a very solemn thought for Advent.

On reading these words from Malachi, my mind is taken back to the end of October 1958. I remember then looking with disgust and despair at the photograph of a man who was on the front page of all the newspapers; a man in his late seventies, with an absurdly-looking hooked nose, who had just been elected Pope of the Roman Catholic Church. And I felt despair that here was this old, ancient-looking Italian, who was now going to be in charge of that great Christian Communion. And yet, in the four-and-a-half years that John XXIII was the Bishop of Rome, he unlocked a spiritual awakening in that church, affecting other churches, such as had not happened for centuries and could not even be imagined to happen at that time. There was an angel or a messenger of God, there was God at work in the world and in his Church, to cleanse and revive and change it.

At this Advent time we think of God coming into the world in a special way in Jesus Christ. While I was thinking about this, the thought occurred to me that the difference between running the world and ruining the world in the words 'run' and 'ruin', is one letter, the letter 'I'. Our desire is to run the world without God, and that works out with us ruining the world. Christmas is the time when we realise that we cannot keep God out of the world that he has made. We celebrate his coming. And this is not like the coming of a schoolteacher back to a class of naughty schoolchildren who have been playing about while the teacher is away – suddenly they have to behave themselves and be good because the teacher has unexpectedly come back. The coming of God in Jesus Christ is the coming of someone who is all that we long for and hope for with regard to a new and better world, and for new and better selves to be part of that world. And so as we think about angels and as we think about coming, as we think about Christmas, let this be our Advent prayer:

> Come, Lord, into our lives. Come into our churches. Come into our world, that we may see you at work and that we may know you more deeply and more truly as the *living* God.

# *Water into wine*

*This beginning of miracles did Jesus in Cana of Galilee, and manifested his glory; and his disciples believed on him*
**John 2:11**

ST. ANDREW'S UNITED REFORMED CHURCH, SHEFFIELD
18TH JANUARY 2004

In what way did Jesus manifest his glory, and what was it his disciples believed about him? Here is George Stanhope, Dean of Canterbury Cathedral at the beginning of the eighteenth century, expressing a point of view that we also had in our first hymn, a very popular hymn for Epiphany-tide.[15] He wrote this:

> This was the first instance which Jesus gave of his divine power and it produced its intended effect by confirming the faith of those disciples who had lately come to him. By the expression "manifested forth his glory", we are to understand that Christ, by the miracles which he performed, plainly proved his power to be divine.[16]

I must confess that I am worried by this statement, for three reasons. The first is a theological and pastoral one. How are we to think of Jesus? Is Jesus a sort of supernatural being in human disguise, going around doing things that are quite beyond human capability, such as (as we heard in the Gospel reading) changing large quantities of water presumably into the same large quantities of wine?[17] If that is how we are to think of Jesus, it seems to me also to affect how we think of our discipleship and following of Jesus. I do not, in any way, suggest that Jesus is anything like Adolf Hitler or Joseph

---

[15] Cp. the second verse of 'Songs of thankfulness and praise': Manifest at Jordan's stream,/Prophet, Priest and King supreme;/And at Cana wedding-guest/In thy Godhead manifest;/Manifest in power divine,/Changing water into wine;/Anthems be to thee addrest,/God in man made manifest.

[16] Quoted in G. D'Oyly and R. Mant, *Notes Explanatory and Practical to the Authorised Version of the Holy Bible*, London: SPCK, 1848, pp.1083-4.

[17] The six water pots will have held around 120 gallons of water.

Stalin. But when we think of what following those people meant in the twentieth century, it meant blind obedience, the following of a figure that was remote and almost god-like in the achievements and the strengths that they were supposed to have. Is that what Christian discipleship is about? Following someone who has great powers that we could never hope to match, and looking up to him as one set upon a pedestal? I must confess that it does not help me very much.

The second thing that bothers me is that if Jesus performed the miracles in order to help people to believe in him, this goes against an enormous amount of what we have in the Bible. The Bible makes it quite clear that miracles are a slippery slope when it comes to creating faith. One of my favourite parts of the Bible are those chapters in Exodus and Numbers where the Israelites are freed from Egypt and wander through the Wilderness. These are foundation stories, which tell us what the people of God is really like. The astonishing thing about these stories is that all the miracles that are performed by God do not help the faith of these people one little bit. According to the way the story is presented they see the Ten Plagues in Egypt, they cross the Red Sea as on dry land, in the Wilderness water comes from the rock, and they are fed with quails and the manna. Yet they still cannot believe! That generation, indeed, is destined in the story not to enter the Promised Land because, after all these miracles, they still ask the question, "Is the Lord with us, or not?"[18] In his own ministry, on occasions when Jesus is asked to give a sign, or to work some miracles that would help people believe in him, he refuses to do so.[19]

---

[18] Exodus 17:7

[19] Luke 11:29-32

I have left until the third point to tell you that I am one of those people who find it very difficult to know what to make of Jesus converting a large amount of water into a large amount of wine. It isn't that I don't believe in miracles; I do. I think God works marvellously and unexpectedly in the world and in human lives, and that we catch glimpses of that from time to time. But this sort of miracle bothers me a great deal. Perhaps I am not the only person here this morning who has that feeling, and if any of you are willing to join me in being slightly ill-at-ease, at least we have one good ally in the form of the great bishop of the Early Church, St Augustine, who was bishop in North Africa in the early fifth century. Augustine explained this miracle in terms of the speeding up of a natural process.[20] He made the point that if you can convert water into wine with the help of a few vines, a bit of sunshine, some pruning and pressing of the grapes, then perhaps this is how it happened, in a speeded-up natural process. I don't believe a word of that! But at least it shows that someone such as Augustine, who had a massive intellect and was one of the great theologians of his era, had difficulties with this story, and so I don't feel quite so bad when I put myself in his company; and perhaps you don't feel quite so bad either.

Did Jesus change water into wine? I am afraid that I cannot answer this question for you. Short of a time-machine to go back to the event, I cannot tell you or convince you whether or not Jesus changed the water into wine. It may be that we are going to have to leave it there. Research has indicated that when it comes to miracles there are three types of person:

---

[20] A. Smitmans, *Das Wunder von Kana. Die Auslegung von Joh, 1-11 bei den Vätern und heute*, Tübingen, 1966.

people who can believe almost anything, those people who can believe almost nothing, and people in the middle who find they are not quite sure.[21] Perhaps there are some here today who have no difficulty in accepting the miracle; that's splendid, and I don't want to disagree with you at all. There may be some people who find it quite impossible to believe it; you have my sympathies. I am somewhere in the middle. I am not quite sure. Yet I want to try and talk about this story in a different way - it may help just a little bit with the third point, but it will certainly address the other two points.

So let us come back to the question: in what way did Jesus manifest his glory, and what was it that his disciples believed? We have recently been singing one of our very popular carols, *Once in royal David's city*, and here we have a picture of Jesus that is rather different from the idea of the semi-divine being, simply in human disguise, with which I started. Instead, Jesus is described by Mrs Alexander in these familiar words:

> For he is our childhood's pattern,
> Day by day like us he grew;
> He was little, weak, and helpless,
> Tears and smiles, like us, he knew;
> And he feeleth for our sadness,
> And he shareth in our gladness.

Those well-known words give us a different idea. They tell us of a Jesus who is fully and truly human in the way that we are. Although I don't want to rule out the possibility that he had powers that enabled him to do marvellous works, what I want

---

[21] Cp. the chapter entitled 'Freedom of Thought' in P. Radin, *Primitive Man as Philosopher*, New York: Dover Publications, 1957, pp.53-62.

to say is this, and I'll say it twice because it is a crucial point: **His power had to do not with the extra-ordinary that is** *beyond* **our abilities. His power had to do with the ordinary that should be** *within* **our abilities, but is mostly not.**

What do I mean by that? I mean that the power of Jesus was his capability of getting alongside people, of getting alongside the outcast, of getting alongside people who thought they had no hope or future, and that this enabled them to have hope in themselves, enabling them to have hope in God. This ability to be completely dedicated to the will of God, and to be completely dedicated to the needs of others, is something that ought to be within our capabilities as human beings, but mostly is not. That is where I want to locate the true power of Jesus, and if we look at the story in this way, all sorts of things begin to make sense. Insofar as the whole question of Christian discipleship is concerned, what we gain is not the exalted leader up there on his pedestal beyond our capabilities. He is the One who comes alongside us. One of the definitions of the nature of God that I particularly like is as follows. If you ask, "What is God like?" the answer is, "God is like a man on a cross who is alongside two other people who are on a cross."[22] That shows something of the closeness to Jesus that this approach brings us and, to me, makes possible a discipleship that is much more meaningful.

If it is true that the writer of this Gospel had as one of his sources something called "The Book of Signs" which had these miracles in it, and he used it as a source (although I must be

---

[22] Cp. H.R.L. Sheppard, *Two Days Before. Simple Thoughts about our Lord on the Cross*, London: SCM Press, 1924, pp.30-31.

careful here, because the academic is getting the better of the preacher), the interesting thing about the story is the way in which this miracle is played down.[23] First of all, we have the words of Jesus to his mother, "Woman, what have you to do with me?" Scholars, and especially Catholic scholars, have spilled gallons of ink trying to prove that Jesus was not being harsh here, but I think he was![24] I think the way the story is presented is meant to show that Jesus did not want to have to do a miracle.

Secondly, according to the story, if you look at it very closely, the only people who know that water has been changed into wine are the servants. Not even the disciples, apparently, seem to know, or at least if they do know, the text doesn't say so. When the steward of the feast says to the bridegroom, "You have kept the best wine until now," the bridegroom has done nothing of the sort! The bridegroom has no idea what has been going on; and we have a great deal of irony in the way this story is told: that the people who think they are in control of the situation (the chief steward and the bridegroom) are not. The only people who know what is really going on are the servants, who do what Jesus tells them. I think, therefore, that John is wanting to present the miracle in a way that plays down the idea that Jesus is in some way a divine superhuman figure, simply disguised as a human being. Perhaps it is no accident that later on in this same chapter, John 2, Jesus is

---

[23] On 'The Book of Signs' see R.E. Brown, *The Gospel according to John* (Anchor Bible), London: Geoffrey Chapman, 1971, p. xxix.

[24] See R.E. Brown, *The Gospel according to John*, p.99: 'This is not a rebuke, nor an impolite term, nor an indication of a lack of affection. It was Jesus' normal, polite way of addressing women.'

asked for a sign and refuses to give it, saying simply and enigmatically that he will destroy the Temple and rebuild it in three days.[25]

Having quoted an Anglican divine at the beginning of this sermon to criticise him, let me now quote another Anglican divine, who, if I am not being too patronising, seems to me to have got it right. This is George Henry Law, Bishop of Bath and Wells in the early part of the nineteenth century. He says this:

> His miraculous works were no less evident signs of mercy, goodness, generosity than of power, and equally adapted to convince men's understandings and engage their affections as to remove their maladies or to relieve their wants. This, his first public miracle, was nothing more than a becoming act of kindness and humanity in preventing the confusion of a poor relation by a very seasonable supply of what was wanting in his entertainment.[26]

What I would like to say, then, is this: the glory that Jesus manifested, and that led to the faith of his disciples, was *not* the power to change quantities of water into wine, but was the goodness, the kindness, and the humanity in entering into a human situation, and preventing it from becoming a disaster. Think of what would have been said among her neighbours, "Oh yes… you remember that at her wedding they didn't have any wine – what a disaster it was!" If we can begin to approach our discipleship in this way, I think we can not only make better sense of the story, but we can also have a better

---

[25] John 2:18-19.

[26] Quoted in D'Oyly and Mant, *Notes Explanatory and Practical*, p.1084.

sense of what the Kingdom of God is about - a kingdom of right relationships, affecting the ordinary things of life.

I could stop there, but perhaps you will allow me just two or three more minutes to say one more thing. One of the punch-lines in this passage is as follows: "You have kept the best wine until now" (which of course the bridegroom hasn't, but that doesn't matter). Over the centuries, Christian interpreters have done all sorts of things with this saying. The one I like best of all is this: that there are many walks of life in which we become interested in something, and yet we quickly grow out of it, we exhaust it, we become bigger than it. Christian faith, the Christian life, and Christian discipleship, truly understood and truly entered into, are a continuous process of the discovery of things that not only satisfy, but challenge and lead us further on. The words, "You have kept the best wine until now," are words about continual discovery. And, of course, I believe that one day, when we have finished our Christian pilgrimage, we will experience something which will lead us to say, as we enter the divine presence,

"You have kept the best wine until now."

# Honouring John the Baptist

*Among those that are born of women there is not a greater prophet than John the Baptist.*
**Luke 7:28**

ST JOHN THE BAPTIST, BAMFORD, DERBYSHIRE
GIVEN AT THE PATRONAL FESTIVAL
27TH JUNE 2004

"Lord, teach us to pray, as John also taught his disciples to pray", are words that you will find at the beginning of Luke 11. It is easy to forget that Jesus was once a disciple of John the Baptist. Indeed, at least several of the first followers of Jesus were also disciples of John the Baptist. Peter, Andrew, Philip and Nathaniel had met Jesus as disciples of John the Baptist before he began his own ministry and called them by the lakeside in Galilee. The impact that John the Baptist made upon Jesus was so great that, in his teaching, Jesus referred more often to John the Baptist than to anyone else. He said:

> "Among those that are born of women there is not a greater prophet than John the Baptist; but he that is least in the kingdom of God is greater than he" (Luke 7:28).

Or another saying,

> "John the Baptist came neither eating bread, nor drinking wine; and ye say, 'He hath a devil'. The Son of man is come eating and drinking; and ye say, 'Behold, a gluttonous man and a winebibber, a friend of publicans and sinners!" (Luke 7:33-34).

The fact that Jesus and some of his own disciples had all been followers of John the Baptist is the background to the words with which I began: "Lord, teach us to pray, as John also taught his disciples." They were obviously thinking back to those times, and they were remembering that one of the striking things about John the Baptist was that he taught his disciples to pray, and they wanted the same with regard to Jesus. In response, Jesus teaches his disciples the prayer that we shall be using later on, what we call the Lord's Prayer.

But what did John teach his disciples to pray? Alas, we are not told, but I want to approach this by talking about two things. First of all, John's own preaching, and, secondly, something about prayer that will perhaps get us to where we want to be. John was a preacher of judgement - a very striking and vivid preacher. He compares the nation to a rotten and diseased tree earmarked for felling. The axe has already been raised and is about to strike the root of the tree, to bring it crashing down. Once the tree has been felled, good parts of it, if there are any, will be rescued and used for something else, while the remainder will be confined to be burnt (Luke 3:9). That does not sound, particularly in the modern world, like a very appealing message. It sounds very much like the Old Testament, and we say that surely Jesus comes to take us beyond that. Hellfire preachers belong, so it seems, to a bygone age. Yet I want to compare John with hellfire preachers of bygone ages, because there is a very important difference between hellfire preachers and Old Testament prophets, John among them. Hellfire preachers – and I hope I am not being unfair to them – have spoken mostly about individuals and the fate awaiting individual men and women, and have offered a way of escaping from the hellfire and judgement that is waiting to come. The preacher, usually *himself*, has reached the rather fortunate position of being exempt from this coming judgement, and is offering other people a way to escape it also. That is quite different from Old Testament prophets, and John among them. For although, of course, they are concerned with what individuals do, or do not do, their sense of coming judgement is directed against the nation, its corruption and its unworthinesses. Old Testament prophets, John among them, do not regard this judgement as something from which they wish to escape. They are part of the nation, and if the judgement falls upon the nation, it falls upon them also. But then there is a further point, that this is not something to be feared, not in the sense of a cringing fear, but something to be hoped for, because if the prophets, and John among them, look for a renewal of the nation following the judgement, they want to be part of this. They proclaim judgement, not out of some sense that they are going to be exempt from some horrible fate that is awaiting everybody else; they look forward to judgement and justice, because that is part of the way in which the just rule of God comes into being. If we follow that line, we can understand why it is that, in the Psalms, we have the psalmists looking forward to the coming judgement of God:

> Let the heavens rejoice, and let the earth be glad; let the sea make a noise, and all that therein is; let the field be joyful, and all that is in it! Then shall all the trees of the wood rejoice before the LORD. For he cometh, for he cometh to judge the earth; and with righteousness to judge the world, and the people with his truth.[27]

Surely there is something here with which we can connect. Is there anybody here this morning who can be satisfied with the world as it is, with its unfairnesses, its double standards, its injustices, its weaknesses and its ignorances? Can any of us here be satisfied with ourselves as we are? After all, a few moments ago we said together a form of confession before God. And so if we long, as I hope we do, for a better world, and ourselves as better people as part of that better world, then surely the judgement of God is not something that we should fear, but something that we should want; not something from which we would wish to escape, but

---

[27] Psalm 96:11-13

something of which we would hope to be part, if we can be better people in a better world. To that extent, therefore, the message of John the Baptist, and his message of coming judgement, is one that is not something to be confined to the idea of outdated hellfire preachers, but something that ought to correspond to our deepest hopes and aspirations.

Now that takes me to my next step, which is to say something about prayer. One of my favourite definitions of prayer is this: prayer is the attempt to see things from the standpoint of God's will and purposes. Now, that is very different from the way in which, in our human weakness, we often pray, which could be said to be our attempt to get God to see things from the point of view of our wills and priorities. I am not saying that is necessarily wrong. As human beings we have our weaknesses; we find ourselves in situations, especially of illness, where things are beyond any kind of human hope, and in those circumstances we turn fervently to God in prayer. And God, in his mercy, but not necessarily according to our orders and our expectations, can answer those prayers marvellously and astonishingly. But the most fundamental idea of prayer is this: it is our attempt to see things from the perspective of *God's* will and purposes. The truest prayer is the prayer that we should be drawn into God's will and purposes, and carry them out whatever the cost.

That brings us very close to the kind of prayer that I think John would have taught his disciples. If John's message is one of the coming judgement, which is to be welcomed, then his view of prayer is not that it is trying to persuade God somehow to fulfil *our* desires. It is a prayer that reality should be conformed to God's will and purpose. I like to think the baptism which John invited his listeners to undergo was not some form of attempt to undergo a rite of passage that would enable them to escape the coming judgement, but rather a request for an acted prayer; a prayer in which, by undergoing baptism, they identified themselves with that coming judgement and gave their assent to wanting to be part of that coming judgement, because it was the just judgement of God to bring about a better world. It would not surprise me if those parts of the Lord's Prayer which say, "Thy kingdom come, Thy will be done, in earth as it is in heaven", have their roots in John the Baptist. And of course we find the perfect example of prayer in the Garden of Gethsemane, when our Lord says,

> "If it be possible, let this cup pass from me. Nevertheless, not as I will, but as thou wilt." [28]

Now, I am conscious that so much more could be said this morning, and that I have said nothing about the Cross and Resurrection of Jesus, and the hope that they bring us for the mercy of God and the faith that comes with that mercy. But a long time ago I learned that you cannot say everything in one sermon, and it is a mistake to try. If you remember anything from what I have said this morning, I hope it will be two things. First, that what the disciples of Jesus who had been with John remembered most about him was that John taught his disciples to pray. The other thing I would like you to remember is that prayer, most profoundly, is our wish to see things from the perspective of God's will and purposes, our desire to be drawn into God's will and purposes, and to live and act accordingly.

---

[28] Matthew 26:39

# Fools for Christ

*The children of this world are in their generation wiser than the children of light.*
**Luke 16:8**

"He's so heavenly-minded that he's no earthly use." I am sure many of you have heard that saying about some Christian or church-going person; someone whose head seems to be so much in the clouds that, when it comes to practical and ordinary things, they seem to be hopeless. This sort of thinking, that one of the troubles with Christian and church people is that they are too heavenly-minded, has often affected the way in which today's Gospel has been understood - "The children of this world are wiser than the children of light" – the idea therefore being, if only church people could be a little bit more worldly!

But does it mean that? Our difficulty is that we do not know whether Jesus was being serious, whether he was being sarcastic or whether he was saying, "Look, I wish I had a few more disciples around me who could manage practical things" (though the fact that among their number was a tax-collector and fishermen, and goodness knows what else, makes you think that they might have had a bit of skill in the practical things of life). So perhaps Jesus was being sarcastic and saying, "OK, if things go wrong, put your trust in the way that the world works" – this is, after all, what the story is about – "and then see what happens"? Well, I do not want to enter into this debate. I think I favour the view that Jesus was being sarcastic, rather than serious; but over against these words, "The children of this world are wiser than the children of light", I want to set some words from Paul:

> The wisdom of this world is foolishness with God.
> If any man among you seemeth to be wise … let him become a fool.

And a little later on in I Corinthians:

We are fools for Christ's sake.[29]

I do not know whether the world would be a better place if the Church and Christians were more worldly, but I am sure of one thing: that the world would be a much poorer place if there were not people who had been, and still are prepared to be, fools for the sake of Jesus Christ.

As someone who has spent his whole life teaching and researching the Old Testament, I would want to take this idea right back to those fools of God, the Old Testament prophets. Jeremiah is sufficient of a fool to think that God is telling him not to marry, not to have a family – a kind of self-denial which in his society was much despised. Jeremiah was fool enough to think God was saying to him that, when Jerusalem was being besieged by the armies of Babylon, he should go and say to the people, "God is not going to fight for this holy city. God is going to let it fall." That foolishness on the part of Jeremiah led among other things to his being denounced as a traitor, being taken prisoner, and being put down into what must have been a ghastly cistern, completely dark with mud and human excrement underfoot.[30]

There is another brand of fools for the sake of Christ, the people we call the martyrs, who were fool enough to maintain their allegiance to Christ and to suffer for it. One of the very earliest we know about is a very old man named Polycarp, who was Bishop of Smyrna. Round about the year 155-156 this

---

[29] 1 Corinthians 3:19; 1 Corinthians 3:18; and 1 Corinthians 4:10 respectively.

[30] Jeremiah 38:6

old man was brought before the Roman Governor and ordered to curse Christ, to which he replied, "Eighty-six years have
I served him; he has done me no wrong. How can I blaspheme
my King who has saved me?"[31] Or we can come closer to our
own times. In the 1930s, when Hitler came to power, there was
a young theologian named Dietrich Bonhoeffer, who utterly
opposed Nazism. On an early occasion when the storm-
troopers came to one of his services, carrying their flags with
the swastika emblazoned on it, and remembering that in
German, the word "swastika" is *das Hakenkreuz* ("broken
cross"), he told these people in no uncertain terms that they
had to choose either the Cross on which Jesus Christ had died,
or the broken cross, but they could not have both and could
not pretend the two were in any way equal. Understandably,
that sort of behaviour meant Bonhoeffer was put under sur-
veillance. In 1939, at the outbreak of war, Bonhoeffer was in
the United States. His friends pleaded with him to stay there
and not to go back to Germany, but Bonhoeffer knew that his
duty as a fool for Christ was to go back. On his return, he ran
an illegal theological college, training men for the ministry
who were also opposed to Nazism, and indeed even passed
secrets to the British Government by meeting Bishop George
Bell of Chichester in Sweden. Not surprisingly, Bonhoeffer
was arrested and imprisoned, and on 9 April 1945, less than a
month before the end of the war, he was executed in a brutal
and vicious way in the concentration camp at Flossenbürg. Yet
the writings of that man have had a great impact, and
especially the book he wrote in 1937, which has the English
title, *The Cost of Discipleship* - all the more telling because here

---

[31] 'The Martyrdom of Polycarp' in J.Stevenson (ed.) *A New Eusebius. Documents illustrative of the history of the Church to A.D. 337*, London: SPCK, 1957, p.21

was someone who not only wrote about the cost of disciple-ship, but was himself prepared to pay the cost of discipleship as a fool for Christ.

One could speak about a great many more examples, but I want to ask the question *why* people are prepared to become fools for Jesus Christ? The most important answer to this question, of course, is that they are following the example of Christ himself, because Christ, in the language that we shall use in the Creed in a minute, is the One "who for us men and for our salvation came down from heaven", or as in the great hymn in Philippians puts it:

> Who, being in the form of God, thought it not robbery to be equal with God: But made himself of no reputation, and took upon him the form of a servant.[32]

That is the first, and most important, reason why people have been prepared to make themselves fools for the sake of Jesus Christ.

But there is at least one other thing to say, and I want to say it in connection with the fact that this week I am thinking about the fortieth anniversary of my Ordination, which took place on 20 September 1964 in Durham Cathedral. I am thinking of the events that led up to that. Now, let me make it quite clear: in no sense am I suggesting that I should be thought of in terms of a Jeremiah, or a Polycarp, or a Bonhoeffer – these are great people who paid the ultimate price, and what I have done is insignificant in comparison. But one of the things that

---

[32] Philippians 2:6-8

set me on the path to Ordination was this discovery: that God was not an idea, or an argument, or a proposition; but that God was a *living* God, active in the world, and active in my own life. I only caught one or two glimpses of that, but those glimpses were sufficient to convince me that God was active in my life, guiding me through things that happened, people I met, things I read, and then – at one important point – calling me to Ordination. That is desperately important, the sense of God as the *living* God, and not just simply an idea, or an argument, or a proposition. For, while people may be willing to make themselves fools for someone they know to be a living God, are they so ready – perhaps sometimes they are – to lay down their lives for simply an idea, or an argument, or a proposition?

Now, let us get back to where I started, those opening words in the Gospel: "The children of this world are in their generation wiser than the children of light." No doubt they are, but the challenge that Paul gives to us is this: "If any man among you seemeth to be wise, let him become a fool, for the wisdom of this world is foolishness with God." As Paul says,

"We are fools for the sake of Christ."

# Is religion a private matter?

*Put on the new man, which after God is created, in righteousness and true holiness*
**Ephesians 4:24**

BEAUCHIEF ABBEY
NINETEENTH SUNDAY AFTER TRINITY
22ND OCTOBER 2006

The news this past week has been preoccupied with whether or not Muslim women should be allowed to wear veils in public. I do not want to talk about this subject as such, except that it links with something in today's Epistle from Ephesians 4. For what it is worth, my opinion on veils is that I find no difficulty with women wearing headscarves. I do, however, find it difficult to cope with dress that covers everything except a person's eyes, and I would add that such dress is in fact rare in Jordan, Syria and Israel/Palestine, Arab countries of which I have some experience.

What has particularly annoyed me this week, however, in the discussions I have heard on the radio, is the assertion that religion is essentially a private matter; that what people do at home or in churches or mosques is their own business, and that these things should not intrude into public life. Such a view is misleading. Christianity, at any rate, is part of the public scene whether people know and like this or not, and I want to talk about it in some detail.

I have spent over thirty years of my life teaching theology and the Bible. I have not been working in the cocooned safety of a seminary or theological college, but in hard-nosed, secular universities. People used to ask me what my mission was as a priest working in the University of Sheffield, and I used to answer that it was to show that Biblical Studies was as demanding and rigorous an intellectual discipline as anything else taught and researched in the university. Over the past two thousand years in general, and the last two hundred years in particular, no set of documents, religious or otherwise, has been subjected to more sustained critical examination than the Bible. No religious prophets have had their words or their lives subjected to such rigorous critical scrutiny over the past two hundred years as the prophets of the Old Testament. No founder of a major world religion has had his life and teaching subjected to such sustained rigorous critical examination, especially over the past two hundred years, as Jesus.

This has come about because it was in Christian Europe that the intellectual movement we call the Enlightenment had its origins, and while it has become fashionable in some circles to denigrate the Enlightenment, I am on the whole a supporter of the Enlightenment. It swept away superstitions and subjected human culture to critical examination. It laid the foundations for modern scientific discovery. Any of us here who have benefited from modern medicine, whether through surgical operations or treatment with new drugs, are benefitting from what was begun at the Enlightenment; *and it is this same use of critical, scientific reason, that has been applied to the Bible and to the life and teaching of Jesus.* The result of this is that the Bible and the life of Jesus are now better understood than ever before, and that their integrity has been enhanced, not destroyed. All this has been done publicly, in institutions of learning open to public scrutiny and review.

All this is largely unknown to a general public that can turn the ludicrous nonsense in Dan Brown's 'The Da Vinci Code' into a best seller. The impression given in that book, that Christianity has from the beginning been a cover-up, could hardly be further from the truth. In fact, Christianity has been open to the most rigorous academic examination. All this is also, alas, largely unknown to the Christian churches, whose leaders prefer to think that most churchgoers have a 'simple faith' that should not be disturbed by asking critical questions. In my experience, churchgoers are intelligent people who want to be helped to think through the difficult questions raised by the Bible and their faith. In this they have much support from the Bible itself, which is not afraid to confront unanswerable questions such as why the wicked apparently prosper and the righteous apparently suffer. The Book of Job is a magnificent endorsement of the fact that God wishes us to ask questions and to argue with and about him.

No other religion has been subjected to such rigorous critical scrutiny as Christianity and no other religious texts have been studied so critically as those of the Bible. This is not to say that other religions and their texts do not contain truth and valuable things; but they have not been critically and publicly tested in the way that Christianity and the Bible have been. To those who say that religion is a private matter to be kept out of public life I have to reply that Christianity is already part of public life and that what it is concerned about – the kind of world in which we live and what it means to be human – are not matters of merely private concern. Christianity is concerned with truth; truth that is prepared to be subjected to public critical scrutiny.

Should Christians wear distinctive dress? The answer is that, historically, some of them have and some still do. If we had lived in a mediaeval town such as York or Norwich we would have been familiar with Benedictine monks in their black habits and Franciscan friars in their brown habits. The canons of Beauchief would have been familiar in their white habits. In the seventeenth century Quakers wore distinctive dress and in the nineteenth century the founder of the Salvation Army, William Booth, expected members to dress distinctively, at least on Sundays.

This is a matter about which we shall have to make up our minds individually but, and this brings me to today's Epistle from Ephesians 4, there is a sense in which all Christians wear something distinctive. The writer speaks of putting off 'the old man, which is corrupt according to the deceitful lusts' and of putting on 'the new man, which after God is created in righteousness and true holiness'. The Greek verbs translated 'putting off' and 'putting on' are those used in connection with clothing, and may refer to the baptismal practice of removing one's clothes prior to entering the waters of baptism and of putting on new garments after having been symbolically identified with Christ's death and rising - that is, if this practice known from later times was already in operation in the late 1st century. Whether or not it was, the idea of putting on new clothes to symbolise one's status before God can already be found in the Parable of the Prodigal Son. When the prodigal returns, a pathetic and miserable creature, he is nonetheless, from his father's point of view, one who was dead and is alive again, who was lost and is found; and the father calls for him to be clothed with the best robe, to indicate that he is once more a son in his father's house.[33] This is also the imagery of Ephesians 4. Christians are those for whom God has symbolically made available a new set of clothes - a new form of being made possible by Christ, in whom the age to come has drawn near to, and is beginning to be operative in, the present age.

Whether or not Christians wear distinctive outward dress, they wear a new humanity made available in Christ. This is why they cannot be happy with the idea that their faith is

---

[33] Luke 15:22-4

something that should be kept secret or confined to what they do in private. As the words with which the offertory is introduced at this service say:

> Let your light so shine before men, that they may see your good works, and glorify your Father which is in heaven.

# Sermon for Ascension Day

*All power is given unto me in heaven and in earth.*
**Matthew 28:18**

ST. MARK'S CHURCH, BROOMHILL, SHEFFIELD
17TH MAY 2007

When I was studying at Theological College I ran a Cub Pack in a local village. We had a football team that played with other Packs in a Saturday league and I would go to shout encouragement and instructions from the touch line. The team never lost, and sometimes won by embarrassingly large margins. There was one exception, however, which was the one Saturday when I couldn't attend because I was taking an examination. The team lost, and when I saw the Cubs the following Thursday they said to me 'We wouldn't have lost if you had been there'.

Whether or not this was true, it was a nice thing for them to say; and it touches on an experience that many of us must have had – that it makes a difference when we are supported by someone we trust and value. Perhaps we have experienced this when taking a music exam or taking part in a music competition; or perhaps it was an anxious visit to the hospital; or we were playing rugby or cricket in a team and were encouraged by the fact that our captain had recovered from injury and was to play with us. Having someone there we trusted and valued made all the difference.

The opposite of this is also true. When that valued person cannot be with us, we are less confident. My cubs said 'We wouldn't have lost if you had been there' and presumably they felt a loss of confidence as they played. This feeling is at its strongest at times of bereavement. Someone we have loved has been taken from us and we are numbed by the fact that part of out life has been ripped away. It takes months or years rather than weeks for the wounds to be healed, for memories to cease to be painful, and we are left with feelings of emptiness and weakness.

This is how the first disciples of Jesus must have felt immediately after the crucifixion. Part of their lives had been ripped from them; their hopes and visions had been torn apart. And then something happened that transformed their lives. Whatever we understand by the resurrection and ascension of Jesus – and experts may disagree about what happened and how we are to understand the stories concerning these things in the New Testament – it cannot be doubted that the disciples were astonished to feel themselves to be empowered. Their sadness was turned to joy, their timidity to courage and their uncertainty to conviction; and they were convinced that it was God who had made these things possible.

No less remarkable than this feeling of empowerment was the message that they felt compelled to proclaim – that all authority in heaven and on earth had been given by God to the one who had suffered and died on the cross, the one who had lived a simple life among them and who had drawn particularly close to the outcasts and the marginalised. This meant all human values had been turned on their head – that greatness could no longer be understood in human terms but only in terms of the one who said that to be greatest of all was to be the servant of all. And this was a message of hope for all who sought a new and better world, because it meant the undermining of those human ideas of greatness and authority that were the cause of so much division and wickedness in the world.

It is important to remember at Ascensiontide that the language in our hymns, prayers and services about greatness, power, authority and glory cannot and must not be understood in human terms, but only in terms of the values proclaimed and lived out by the one who died on the cross.

I have felt for a long time that in the Church of England we are badly served by the authorised services and prayers that we have to use at this time of the year. I have particular problems with the Collect for the Sunday after the Ascension, a prayer specially composed for the first English Prayer Book of 1549 and which has survived various liturgical reforms more or less unscathed. In its form in *Common Worship* it reads as follows:

> O God the king of glory, you have exalted your only Son Jesus Christ with great triumph to your kingdom in heaven: we beseech you, leave us not comfortless, but send your Holy Spirit to strengthen us and to exalt us to the place where our Saviour Christ is gone before.

The difficulty I have with this is that it is in danger of creating the very thing it is praying to prevent and suggesting to us that in fact we *have* been left as orphans. It is in danger of creating what I call 'the doctrine of the Real Absence of Christ from the world', implying that we have to be content with a second best, the Holy Spirit (a concept which may be hard to grasp, especially when in the past we were encouraged to think the Holy Spirit was only really in operation when bishops were present, and doing things! ).

We badly need to find ways of expressing in theology and worship the great insights of the New Testament about the exaltation of Jesus; and here are some suggestions. Joseph Ratzinger, long before he became a cardinal and a pope, wrote

> it would be a misunderstanding of the Ascension if some sort of temporary absence of Christ from the world were to be inferred from it. The "sitting on the right hand of the Father" of which Scripture speaks...signifies rather the human Jesus' participation in the kingly power of God, and so precisely his

authoritative presence in the world and among those he has made his own. (Cf Matthew 28:20)

So we can be reassured that Ratzinger, at least when he wrote these lines, was aware that Jesus had completely subverted human ideas of greatness and authority, he said later in the article,

the cross becomes paradoxically a sign of the exaltation of the Lord in this world.[34]

Here is Brian Wren in a hymn about the exaltation of Jesus:

Christ is alive! No longer bound
to distant years in Palestine,
but saving, healing, here and now
and touching every place and time.

Not throned afar, remotely high,
untouched, unmoved by human pains,
but daily, in the midst of life,
our Saviour in the Godhead reigns.[35]

Here is an older prayer:

'Glory to our ascended Lord, that he is with us always; glory to the Word of God, going forth conquering and to conquer; glory to him who has led captivity captive, and gone to prepare a place in his Father's house for us, the author and finisher of our faith'.[36]

---

[34] J. Ratzinger, 'Ascension of Christ' in K. Rahner (ed.), *Encyclopedia of Theology. A Concise Sacramentum Mundi*, London: Burns & Oates, 1975, pp. 46-7.

[35] B. Wren, 'Christ is alive! Let Christians sing' 260 in *Rejoice and Sing*, Oxford: Oxford University Press, 1991.

[36] Taken from *New Every Morning*, London: The British Broadcasting Corporation, 1936, p. 77.

I have been asked to mention that this is Christian Aid Week - the fiftieth anniversary of the first Christian Aid Week. I find it inspiring in today's world of political correctness where some local authorities think 'Inter-faith' means 'not Christian', that money is being collected in the name of *Christian* Aid from people of no faith or faiths such as Islam and Hinduism as well as from Christians. This can be justified in terms of what I have been saying about the meaning of the exaltation of Jesus. His subversion of human values gives us hope for a better world, a world from which poverty and suffering are eliminated, and part of the practical way in which we help Christ's 'reign' to be realised is by action to combat poverty and suffering. Provided that we act as a serving Church, we can with a good conscience challenge people of no faith or other faiths to help work towards the better world which Christ's 'reign' promises.

But another idea which I heard recently, suggested by John Vincent, is that as well as a 'make poverty history' campaign we need a 'make affluence history' campaign. Good as the 'make poverty history' campaign has been, it is difficult to avoid the feeling that politicians and others who support it think that the primary thing is to create wealth, so it can be better distributed to the poor.

In the 1930s and 1940s, Archbishop William Temple and R.H. Tawney were arguing that, from a Christian viewpoint, the creation of wealth could *only* be justified if the reason for doing so was to relieve poverty. They maintained that the existence of affluence for its own sake was incompatible with Christianity. In a radio broadcast in the autumn of 1940 Temple said:

we can only solve the paradox of poverty in the midst of plenty by abolishing the plenty.[37]

Temple had the weight of Christian tradition behind him, from the man on the cross whose life had been led in simplicity, through the many attempts to follow him in the monastic life and other ways.

Ascensiontide presents us with much to think about, and I conclude by adapting, as a prayer for us all, the blessing in the Alternative Service Book for Whitsunday:

> May the Spirit of truth lead us into all truth, give us grace to confess that Jesus Christ is Lord, and to proclaim the word and works of God.

---

[37] Quoted in W.G. Peck 'William Temple as Social Thinker' in W.R. Matthews, et al., *William Temple: An Estimation & an Appreciation*, London: James Clark & Co., 1946, p. 69.

# The search for truth
# and the will to power

*Go and search diligently for the young child; and when ye have found him, bring me word again, that I may come and worship him also.*

**Matthew 3:8**

BEAUCHIEF ABBEY
A SERMON FOR EPIPHANY
6TH JANUARY 2008

The Epiphany story presents us with two possible approaches to life: the Search for Truth and Meaning, and the Will to Power. Those who embark on the search for truth and meaning begin a journey not knowing where it will lead or where it will end. It may lead them to do things they never expected to do; it may lead them to consider ideas quite different from what they have always accepted. It may lead them into danger or even death; yet it will be part of a process of becoming – of becoming what they truly are.

In the New Testament story of the Epiphany the men called in Greek the *magoi* (better translated as wise men rather then kings) set out on a journey not knowing where it will lead or what they will find. It may be a long journey or a short one. They do not know that they may run the danger of incurring the wrath of the great king Herod, or of provoking a political crisis in Judea. When they find what they are looking for, they worship, and offer their gifts. They do not try to possess what they have found, or use it for their own interests. They worship, and offer their gifts. In this regard their action is identical with true love. When true love finds what it is seeking it does not try to dominate it or use it for its own interests. It honours what is loved, and seeks to give to it. Unfortunately, there are counterfeit versions of love in human society, where attempts are made to dominate and manipulate the object of the love. Thus arise the situations in which relationships are ruined and break down.

The will to power has no scruples about dominating and manipulating others. If it wants to learn anything, it will only be so that what is learned can put to use in the gaining and exercise of power. In the Epiphany story Herod is an excellent example of the will to power. He is called 'the Great', and anyone who visits the Holy Land today will see more evidence of his building projects than those of any other ruler of the area before or since. At Caesarea Maritime and you can see remains of the great aqueduct built to bring water from several miles to the north. Go to Jerusalem and to the Western or Wailing Wall, and you will see the enormous stones three feet high that are part of the foundations of Herod's enlargement of the temple. In March 1964 I was lucky to be present at an archaeological congress at Masada, when frescoes were discovered that decorated Herod's private quarters on the three levels on the northern side of that remarkable mound. I could mention other examples of his works such as those at New Testament Jericho, or Herodium or Machaerus. Yet this man, considered great, was pathologically suspicious of those around him, and in his determination to hold on to power at all costs, had two of his sons assassinated and his favourite wife executed, because he suspected they might be a threat to his power. The Epiphany story, according to which Herod had all the boys in Bethlehem aged two and under killed in case one of them was the king sought by the wise men, is certainly not out of character.

Unfortunately, we do not have to look to the past to find examples of the will to power. The people of Kenya are currently suffering greatly because it is believed that the recent presidential election was rigged in order to allow the current president to remain in power. But rigged elections are not unknown nearer to home. Some of you will remember the dispute in the Electrical Trades Union in 1958-61, when a brave man named Les Cannon was able to convince the High Court that elections to offices in the union had been rigged in order to allow the Communist officials to stay in office. Or we can think of the example of Robert Maxwell, who did not scruple to use the pension funds of the Daily Mirror to prop up his ailing financial empire, robbing beneficiaries of what they had saved for their retirement. And we have to be honest and admit that in the church, mediaeval popes and Anglican prince bishops have often resembled king Herod rather than the wise men! Thomas of Canterbury, to whom the foundation of this Abbey is dedicated, was murdered in Canterbury Cathedral because he stood by the truth as he saw it, against the wishes of Henry II.

As Christians we are committed to the search for truth and meaning, not the will to power. It is a journey whose outcome we are not be able to predict; which may lead us to unexpected professions or ideas, or to situations that seem to be against our best interests. But it is a journey that leads us to a point where we want only to worship and offer our gifts.

But the matter does not end there. The journey, the search for truth and meaning is not one-sided. If we are searching for God, the good news is that he is also searching for us. There would be no Christmas or Epiphany story if God were not seeking us, if he were not seeking to bring us to the point where we can worship, and offer our gifts. So we set out on our search for truth and meaning, confident that through God's grace we have found, and shall find, the One who is the Way, the Truth and the Life.

# Putting on Christ

*Put on the new man, which after God is created in righteousness and true holiness.*
**Ephesians 4:24**

BEAUCHIEF ABBEY
EIGHTH SUNDAY AFTER TRINITY
13TH JULY 2008

The sermon that I preached four weeks ago seems to have provoked more than usual interest. For those who could not be here, I compared the Greek idea of the immortal soul with the biblical/Christian view that we are whole persons in the sight of God. The Greek view implies that, when we die, our immortal soul, which we have because we are human, survives death. The biblical/Christian view is that our life is dependent upon God. If there is life beyond death, it is not because we are human and have an immortal soul, but because we are resurrected to new life through a gracious act of God.

After the sermon a month ago, Claire pointed out to me the words in the Prayer of Humble Access: 'that our sinful bodies may be made clean by his body, and our souls washed through his most precious blood' and asked what 'souls' meant in this context. I shall try to answer this in the first part of today's address.

I begin with words that we used at the beginning of the service in Our Lord's summary of the law. Asked to define what was the greatest commandment, Jesus quoted from Deuteronomy 6:4. This is the beginning of a prayer which is as familiar to observant Jews as the Lord's Prayer is to Christians. In its Hebrew version it goes (in my translation)

> Hear, O Israel! The Lord our God, the Lord is one; and thou shalt love the Lord thy God with all thy heart, and with all thy soul and with all thy might.

We need to translate the Hebrew thought-forms if we are to understand this. For the Hebrew, the heart was the seat of the intellect, or the mind. To say that we must love God with all our heart is to say we must love him with our knowledge and our intellect. If this seems strange to us, we must remember that in English we say of someone who has been disappointed in love that they are heartbroken. This is not the same as the Hebrew, but it does ascribe emotional feelings to the heart and presumably comes from a time when this was commonly done in English.

The word translated as 'soul' basically means 'neck'. This can be seen from the opening words of Psalm 69, where the psalmist says (in the older translations) 'Save me O LORD, for the waters are come in even to my soul'. What he means, of course, is that he feels as though waters have risen up to his neck! For the Hebrew, the neck was the seat of the emotions, something that we can appreciate because we say in English 'I had a lump in my throat' when we experience joy or happiness. Translated or understood as 'soul' the word denotes our emotions or feelings. To love God with our soul means to love him with that part of our being that concerns our emotions and our psychology. In the Prayer of Humble Access we pray that our souls may be washed, that is, that those things in our psychological and emotional make-up that need repair may be healed. The third word, 'might' refers to the physical part of our being, and later Jewish interpretation understood it to include our material wealth.

The three terms taken together, heart, soul, and might, refer to our whole being: body, mind, emotions and feelings, creativity, and material possessions. It is God's call for loyalty in every aspect of our lives.

## ( II )

I begin the second part of the address by asking whether any of you have seen the Vivienne Westwood exhibition currently at the Millennium Galleries in Sheffield. What I found interesting about the exhibition was Vivienne Westwood's belief that clothes help us to express what we are or wish to become. In the 1970s she and her husband designed clothes intended to help young people involved in Punk Rock to express this commitment. The idea that clothes help us to express what we are or wish to become is a profoundly biblical view, and has appeared at least three times in the service this morning.

The Epistle from Ephesians spoke of 'putting on the new man' - the idea being that of symbolically putting on a robe provided by God in order to express the new life to which he has called us. The hymn that followed, 'Soldiers of Christ, arise, and put your armour on' invoked the image of Christians dressing themselves in armour provided by God in order to undertake his mission in the world. In the Parable of the Prodigal Son the Father ordered his servants to bring the best robe with which to clothe the returning son.

A most important point is that the robe which God symbolically provides is given at the beginning, not the end of the Christian life. In the next week or so, students at universities and colleges all over the country will be graduating, and wearing for the first time the robes that their hard work and success in examinations will entitle them to wear. The right to wear these robes comes at the end of their endeavours. It is quite different in the Christian life. The robes come at the beginning because God takes us as we are, and in his unfathomable mercy declares us to be his sons and daughters. This is clear in the Parable of the Prodigal Son. The returning son was not a nice person to look at. He was dirty, smelly, unkempt and wearing rags; yet the Father takes him as he is and puts on him a robe to signify that he is his son. The robe marks the beginning of a new life in which he is to become the son whom the Father has declared him to be.

It is the same with us. We are not concerned as Christians to try to save an immortal soul. God takes us as we are with all our faults and failings and declares that we are his sons and daughters. Symbolically he gives us a robe to express that status, a robe that helps us to express what we are and what we seek through God's grace to become. It is God's will to say of each of us that which is said in the parable:

> this my son or my daughter was dead and is alive again; was lost and is found.

# Our search for God
# or God's search for us?

*Where is he that is born King of the Jews? For we have seen his star in the east, and are come to worship him.*
**Matthew 2:2**

BEAUCHIEF ABBEY,
4TH JANUARY 2009

The Epiphany Season is an interesting and quite challenging time in the Church's calendar. It can be squeezed, a bit like a concertina, almost into nothingness. Do you remember last year, with Easter being so early, we only had one Sunday after the Epiphany? In the year 2000 – I didn't remember this; I looked it up, I must admit – we had six Sundays after the Epiphany, because Easter was late. The usual average is three or four Sundays. But it is a season that can pass by unnoticed, and yet it is quite challenging for this reason: the themes and readings which it contains can easily be misunderstood.

Today, for example, we have the much-loved story of the visit of the Wise Men to Jesus in Bethlehem - and where would we be without the artistic representations, the hymns, the carols and the Christmas cards with usually three kings (although the Bible does not tell us how many there were) offering their gifts to Jesus? In this year 2009, this story is, I think, a particularly important one, because we are already beginning to hear much about Charles Darwin, who was born in the year 1809, and whose book, *On the Origin of the Species by Natural Selection*, was published 150 years ago in 1859. The story of the Epiphany is very important, because it tells of the fact that scientists – these men were astrologers, in those days a serious science – are led to the source of that truth. I have said on a number of occasions here in the Abbey that we have nothing to fear as Christians from the scientific or any other investigation of the world in which we live; and I have emphasised before that what is important about Christianity is its willingness to be investigated by critical academic scholarship in a way that is not true of any of the other great religions.

So this story of the Wise Men is important. It gives us the idea of the human search for truth as being something God-given, something God-inspired, and I hope that we shall learn a lot about Darwin and the controversies of the nineteenth century in the year ahead. But then we must make one qualification, because if we look at the Wise Men story carefully, we see that although the Wise Men *are* finally led to God-with-us, they begin their journey by looking for a human, for one who is born King of the Jews. And that, of course, is not what the Christmas message is about. The Christmas message is not about a human search for a baby who is to be born king; the Christmas message is about God-with-us. God was in Christ; God coming to be with us, and to go all the way with us, for our salvation and for the redemption of the world. I suppose we can say: we only find God if God lets himself be found, but then, of course, the Christmas message is that this is precisely what God wants to happen. God comes among us precisely so that we may find him. But we need to put these two things together, and remember that the human search alone will not bring us to God; and it is interesting that in the Greek Church, this festival is not called "Epiphany" (manifestation), but "Theophany", that is, the Manifestation of God.

Now let me get on to the second point of the two that I want to make. The readings that come up in the next three or four weeks all emphasise what I might call the supernatural or superhuman side of Jesus. Next Sunday, the Gospel is about the boy Jesus in the Temple, displaying his astonishing knowledge, far greater than that of the learned men who are there. The following week, we have the story of Jesus changing the water into wine. The week after that there are two miracles: the healing of a leper and of a centurion's servant. On the fourth Sunday in Epiphany, we get the story of Jesus encountering that strange, wild figure who rose among the tombs in the town of Gerasa and whom he heals by driving the demons into a herd of swine. Now, one of the troubles with emphasising what we might call these superhuman aspects of Jesus is that we may forget that he was truly and fully human. This is a mistake that has often been made in the history of the Church, and which can have some bad consequences. There is a hymn - we are not singing it today - sung at Epiphany-tide written by Christopher Wordsworth, who was Bishop of Lincoln in the latter part of the nineteenth century (and he was, incidentally, a firm opponent of Darwin and of any sense of the scientific and critical investigation of the Bible and theology). Wordsworth wrote this hymn, but again it seems to me to overdo the stress on the superhuman side:

Songs of thankfulness and praise
Jesus, Lord, to thee we raise
Manifested by the star
To the sages from afar;
Branch of royal David's stem
In thy birth at Bethlehem;
Anthems be to thee addressed,
God in man made manifest.

Manifest at Jordan's stream,
Prophet, Priest and King supreme;
And at Cana, wedding guest,
In thy Godhead manifest;
Manifest in power divine,
Changing water into wine;
Anthems be to thee addressed,
God in man made manifest.

Manifest in making whole
Palsied limbs and fainting soul;
Manifest in valiant fight,
Quelling all the devil's might ...

And there's more in that vein. One of the troubles with this view is that it overlooks something very important in our understanding of the Gospel narratives when we say that Jesus is truly human and truly divine. The thing missed is this: that when we read the stories of Jesus healing people, Jesus constantly makes the point that it is not so much he who has done the healing, but that God has done the healing through the *faith* of the person involved. "Go your way", says Jesus time and again, "your faith has saved you, your faith has made you whole". And we are told in Mark 6 that when he came to Nazareth, he was not able to do many mighty works there, because of the people's lack of faith.

What this leads to is, that one of the important things about the ministry of Jesus, and one of the ways in which he is truly God, is that he enables people to have faith in God. He enables that faith to be effective in healing. In the case of the first disciples, he enables that faith to be effective in the preaching of the Gospel to the world. Although, of course, there is far, far more to say about what it means to say that Jesus is truly human and truly God than what I have just said, it seems to me that this is something that we must cling to: Jesus is God in the sense that he helps us to have faith in God. He inspires our faith, because he is there as someone we can read about, some-one we can worship, someone we can be drawn to in his preaching, his teaching and in his parables; and that we can do these things when our own faith may be very shaky, when we may not be sure that we are doing the right thing, and yet we can be sure that if we are trying faithfully and honestly to serve Jesus, then we are in touch with God and serving God. This is a side that I would want to stress; not so much the superhuman side of Jesus, but Jesus helping us to have faith in God, and that faith becoming more real.

I sometimes end these addresses of mine with a prayer, and I came across one that I thought would do well for Epiphany-tide and this Sunday:

> O God, who once of old didst reveal thy Son Jesus Christ, to Wise Men studying the face of the heavens, grant us to welcome the revelation of wisdom and science, through which in our own day thou dost make thy name known among us. Reveal thyself again to men and women of learning that through their work the world may come to know thee anew, and may offer new gifts and treasures to the glory of thy name, who art evermore revealed in thy Son, Jesus Christ our Lord. Amen.[38]

---

[38] Collect for Epiphany, Book of Common Prayer

# Quantitative easing: God's version

*The kings of the Gentiles exercise lordship over them; and they that exercise authority upon them are called benefactors. But ye shall not be so: but he that is greatest among you, let him be as the younger; and he that is chief, as he that doth serve.*

**Luke 22:25**

SHEFFIELD CATHEDRAL
MAUNDY THURSDAY
9TH APRIL 2009

One of the interesting things about the first three gospels is that although they received many of the same traditions, they sometimes put them into different orders. All of the first three gospel writers received traditions about the Last Supper and all had traditions about the disciples quarrelling about which of them should be the greatest; only Luke put them together so that the dispute about greatness followed the account of the institution of the Last Supper.

I am very grateful to Luke for doing this. He had the insight to represent the disciples as so clueless about the significance of the Last Supper that they quarrelled among themselves at the conclusion of the meal. If this seems astonishing to us, we have to reflect that we have learned nothing in the two thousand years that have passed since then. Disputes about the Last Supper split the churches at the Reformation, and still do. I was recently invited to conduct a Communion service at a URC church and could not help being aware of the fact that a URC Minister would not be able to conduct a Communion Service in an Anglican church.

I would like, for the moment, to concentrate on the dispute about greatness, about who was to be superior. To be superior means that there must be an inferior; there can be no plus without a minus. The idea that one is superior is not just a personal whim. It is bringing to expression an attitude that is widely shared in society – that one race is superior to another, one nation is superior to another, one class is superior to another, the possession of one type of car is superior to another and that one income bracket is superior to another. This attitude divides societies and means that the inferior people can be regarded as less than fully human. It was this view of what it means to be human that the disciples were invoking as they quarrelled together about which of them should be the greatest.

There are similarities between this world view and the world view that underlies the use of money - a subject at present much on all our minds on account of the credit crisis. Whatever else money is, it is a way of giving concrete expression to a whole series of shared conventions that make life together possible. If I take a five-pound note to a greengrocer and exchange it for fruit and vegetables I assume that he is charging me a fair price for items that are fresh and wholesome. He also assumes that the piece of paper that I give him in return for the fruit and vegetables can be used by him to get further goods or services. My five-pound note depends for its value upon shared meanings that can be translated into concrete things or actions. Many years ago I obtained some inflation marks in Germany, bank notes issued in the 1920s with a face value of, in one case, two million marks. If I took that bank note to my greengrocer he would not exchange it for fruit and vegetables because the piece of paper would have no meaning within our shared conventions. Monopoly money is worthless in the real world, but has value if I play the game of Monopoly and accept the rules governing that game. So far I have mentioned only the good aspects of money – the bonds of trust that underlie its use. In our current financial crisis, that trust has been undermined by greed, fraud, and incompetence. The result of this destruction of trust is that people are losing houses and livelihoods, and we are witnessing the immoral spectacle of governments worldwide coming to the aid of the debts of rich corporations when they find it impossible to do anything to help the much smaller debts of third-world countries.

In the gospels there are numerous instances of money being alluded to as a way of illustrating the message of the Kingdom of God. There are the parables of the Labourers in the Vineyard in which all workers receive the same pay regardless of hours worked, the Unforgiving Servant where the master remits a huge debt owed by a servant only for that servant to pursue a fellow-servant mercilessly for a trifling debt, and the Parable of the Unjust Steward where a steward adjusts what was owed to his master. The Parable of the Pounds or Talents assumes that sums of money entrusted to servants are to be used by them in order to get a bigger return; in the story of the widow's mite the trifle the widow has contributed to the temple offering is seen as greater than the much larger sums contributed by richer people. These and other passages use the figure of money to speak of a sphere of reality quite different from that found in the desire of the disciples for superiority, or the way in which the normal use of money can be destructive of communities. It is the realm represented at the Last Supper, the realm in which God pours his mercy and grace into the world in order to meet our moral and spiritual bankruptcy. This spiritual capital is not cheap. Other writers in the New Testament use images drawn from money to describe it. 'Ye know the grace of our Lord Jesus Christ' says Paul in 2 Corinthians 8:9, 'that, though he was rich, yet for your sakes he became poor, that ye, through his poverty, might be rich.' In 1 Peter 1:18-19 we read that 'ye were not redeemed with corruptible things, as silver or gold... but with the precious blood of Christ, as of a lamb without blemish and without spot'. The very word 'redeemed' is another path into the world of money and reckoning, as it draws on the image of the freedom of slaves or prisoners being purchased with money. In Isaac Watts's famous hymn, the opening lines go:

When I survey the wondrous Cross, on which the Prince of Glory died, my richest gain I count but loss, and pour contempt on all my pride.

The image of money can help us to understand one aspect of meaning of the Lord's Supper. If I have a five-pound note it has no value of itself. It has value only if I use it - if I take it to the greengrocer and exchange it for fruit and vegetables within the context of shared meanings which make our communal life possible. Bread and wine have more value than a five-pound note that is not being used – they can at least be eaten. At our Communion service bread and wine are given new meaning by the narrative of the Last Supper. They become embedded in those shared conventions that make possible our participation in the Kingdom of God, that realm in which God's mercy and grace are extended to us. While remaining bread and wine, they become the means by which God's mercy reaches out to each of us personally, accepting us as we are, affirming us, and challenging us. This happens in spite of our modern versions of the quarrel of the disciples about who should be the greatest. Luke did us a great service by bringing the two themes together.

# On commodifying Jesus

*Then one of the twelve, who was called Judas Iscariot, went to the chief priests and said, 'What will you give me if I betray him to you?' They paid him thirty pieces of silver. And from that moment he began to look for an opportunity to betray him.*
**Matthew 26:14-16**

SHEFFIELD CATHEDRAL
SECOND ADDRESS ON GOOD FRIDAY
10TH APRIL 2009

Judas Iscariot rarely appears in the Gospel narratives without it being added that he was the one who betrayed Jesus. The name 'Judas' has become a way of calling someone a traitor, and I have never met anyone whose first name was Judas. But what did he do that was worse than what the other disciples did? Surely, it was not possible to be worse than Peter, who denied that he had ever known or had anything to do with Jesus. What about Thomas, who said he would not believe that Jesus had risen from the dead unless he could put his finger into the mark of the nails and his hand into the pierced side of Jesus? What about the other disciples who deserted Jesus when he was arrested? What was different about what Judas did to earn him the title of the one who betrayed Jesus?

In recent years attempts have been made to find explanations for the action of Judas. Perhaps he thought he was helping Jesus by bringing matters to a head; perhaps he had become disillusioned with Jesus, wanting to force him into action. I am not going to follow these lines of speculation, but will merely point out that, in agreeing to betray Jesus for money, Judas was turning Jesus into a commodity that could be valued in monetary terms. It does not matter whether thirty pieces of silver was a large or small sum, the point is that Jesus became something that could be traded. In this respect he was put into the same category as millions of human beings who have been denied their right to be persons, and become objects of trade. The most obvious members of this group are slaves who, deprived of their freedom, were bought and sold like any other commodity. But the same fate is shared by many workers in today's world who have become mere statistics in the world of commerce, as its economic imperatives have decreed that enterprises should be 'slimmed down', or 'made more competitive', or 'rationalised' – these phrases being ways of saying that people who may fall victim to such processes were thought of in purely monetary terms. Good Friday is not a time for feeling good, but a time for seeing the consequences of human behaviour in the light of the Cross. To the extent that we take for granted a world in which people are made into tradable commodities we, like Judas, betray Jesus, who became one with those who are seen in monetary terms only.

That this should not be so from the perspective of the Kingdom of God is made clear by the parable of the Labourers in the Vineyard[39]. A householder needs labourers to help him at the time of the grape harvest. At the beginning of the day he hires a number of workers and agrees to pay them the usual daily wage. He then goes out and hires more workers after three, six, nine and eleven hours. There may have been good reasons for this. The arrangement gave him flexibility. He was able to match his workforce to the progress being made. It was also a way of keeping costs down, because it was cheaper than hiring a larger number of workers at the beginning of the day. The climax of the parable comes when the workers are paid, beginning with those who worked only one hour. They receive a full day's wage, a move which angers those who had worked for twelve hours, and who resent being made equal with those who worked for only one hour. While we can appreciate their anger, it has to be said that it made sense only on the assumption that they and their fellow workers were seen as nothing more than providers of labour, which had a monetary value. The fact that some had stood in the market place for eleven hours hoping that they might get work, and wondering how they would face hungry wives and children

---

[39] Matthew 20:1-16

when they returned home empty-handed, was not a factor to be taken into account. It has been said that the economics implied in the parable would be disastrous if applied to the world, and that is no doubt correct; but it is also a judgement on a way of ordering human affairs that decrees that many people will be regarded only in monetary terms, not as people who have needs, aspirations and dependants. In his commentary on Romans, Karl Barth describes the faithfulness of God as expressed in Jesus as his willingness to enter 'within the deepest darkness of human ambiguity' and to abide within it.

> 'Jesus stands among sinners as a sinner; He sets himself wholly under the judgement under which the world is set; He takes his place where God can be present only in questioning about him; He takes the form of a slave'[40]

and, we can add, he becomes a tradable commodity along with millions of others in human history.

There is a sad end to the story of Judas.[41] He attempts to re-deem himself by returning the money he had received for betraying Jesus. The chief priests refuse to accept it, and Judas takes his own life. Why is he apparently outside the mercy of God when the other disciples who betrayed Jesus were forgiven? Was it his misfortune to take his own life before the

---

[40] K. Barth, *The Epistle to the Romans* (translated by E. C. Hoskins), Oxford: Oxford University Press, 1968, p. 97. German original, Die Treue Gottes ist sein Hineingehen und Verharren in der tiefsten menschlichen Fragwürdigkeit und Finsternis...Er stellt sich als Sünder zu den Sündern. Er stellt sich selbst gänzlich unter das Gericht, unter dem die Welt steht. Er stellt sich selbst dorthin, wo Gott nur noch als Frage nach Gott gegenwärtig sein kann. Er nimmt Knechtgestalt an. K.Barth, *Der Römerbrief*, Zürich: Theologischer Verlag, 1999, p. 78.

[41] Matthew 27:3-10

Resurrection? Might Jesus have appeared to Judas as he did to Peter and Thomas? Or perhaps in the world in which people are turned into commodities to be traded and thus depersonalised, there is no place for mercy and forgiveness.

# Barabbas and the celebrity culture

*And they had them a notable prisoner, called Barabbas*
**Matthew 27:16**

SHEFFIELD CATHEDRAL
THIRD ADDRESS ON GOOD FRIDAY
10TH APRIL 2009

How well known was Jesus when he came to Jerusalem for the last week of his life? It is usually assumed he was well known and that this notoriety was reinforced by the reception he received from the crowds on Palm Sunday. This leads preachers to be able to show the fickleness of crowds that shouted 'Hosanna' on Palm Sunday and 'crucify' on Good Friday and who preferred that the murderer Barabbas should be released rather than Jesus. This can make us feel good, as though, if we had been there, we would not have been so irresponsible.

I am not sure this is right. It has been estimated that, at Passover, there were 125,000 visitors to Jerusalem to add to the normal population of around 55,000.[42] Even if we divide these numbers in half, we are left with 90,000 pilgrims and inhabitants, and anyone at all familiar with the traditional route from Bethphage to Jerusalem, will doubt whether 90,000 people could have lined it. In any case, why would they have wanted to? How could they know what was about to happen? The likelihood is that the 'triumphal entry' to Jerusalem was a very small-scale affair, organised by Jesus's followers and looked on with curiosity by bystanders. But did not Jesus teach daily in the temple? Yes, and so did scores of others, probably, in some corner of the great outer courtyard which, according to Acts 2:41, could contain several thousand people. Jesus came from Galilee, a region not noted for producing distinguished teachers, and most of his ministry had been in that area. There would be no reason for the general populace of Jerusalem to know about, or be interested in, the mission

---

[42] J. Jeremias, *Jerusalem zur Zeit Jesu*, Göttingen: Vandenhoeck & Ruprecht, 1958, I, p. 96.

and message of Jesus. Further, if he was largely unknown in Jerusalem, this would explain why Judas needed to betray Jesus and to identify him in the Garden of Gethsemane.

I am going to assume that Jesus was not well known when Pilate offered to release him and that, on the contrary, Barabbas was much better known. He is described, indeed, as notorious and if the suggestion is correct that his crime was not so much murder, as insurrection against Roman rule that involved violence against the ruling power, he would have enjoyed a good deal of popular support and sympathy. What I want to suggest is that Barabbas was what we would call today a celebrity, and that what the crowd was being asked to choose was between a celebrity and someone who was virtually unknown. There was no contest, and in their place, we would have voted for the celebrity.

If this is right, it establishes a link with our world. The sociologist Zygmunt Bauman has suggested the two roles that typify society today are the victim and the celebrity.[43] The victim typifies the compensation culture in which no one can be trusted to work honestly or to make genuine mistakes. The celebrity is the glamorous manifestation of the will to power, whose main achievement is somehow to become well known. As Bauman observes, the celebrity gives little or nothing to his or her followers other than a desire to achieve comparable fame, and demands nothing in return. It is possible to switch loyalty from one celebrity to another without any sense of betrayal, or to admire many celebrities at once. If celebrities are role models, they are missionaries for 'the world of the will to

[43] Z. Bauman, *Liquid Life*, Cambridge: Polity Press, 2005, pp. 49-50

power' - advancement to the top that requires the sacrifice of others, not the sacrifice of oneself for the sake of others.

To the extent that we approve of the world of the celebrity and endorse it with our adulation, we choose Barabbas over against Jesus. Karl Barth has some profound words that are pertinent to this subject

> His [Jesus's] greatest achievement is a negative achievement. He is not a genius, endowed with manifest or even occult powers; He is not a hero or leader of men; He is neither poet nor thinker... He sacrifices to the incomparably Greater and to the invisibly Other every claim to genius and every human heroic or aesthetic or psychic possibility, because there is no conceivable human possibility of which He did not rid Himself. Herein He is recognized as the Christ... In Him we behold the faithfulness of God in the depths of hell. [44]

We know nothing about Barabbas other than his name in the Gospel narratives. It is ironic that he should owe this notoriety to his accidental association with the one who deliberately chose the path that led in the opposite direction from celebrity, to the disgrace, humanly speaking, of a criminal's cross. He thereby exposed 'the world of the will to power' for what it was, and revealed the will to love and mercy of his heavenly Father.

---

[44] K. Barth, *Epistle to the Romans*, p. 97; German original: Er ist auf der Höhe, am Ziel seines Weges eine rein negative Größe: keinesfalls Genie, keinesfalls Träger manifester oder okkulter psychischen Kräfte, keinesfalls Held, Führer, Dichter oder Denker...gerade darin, daß er einem unmöglichen Mehr, einem anschaulichen Andern opfert alle genialen, psychichen, heldischen, ästhetischen, philosophischen, überhaupt alle denkbaren menschlichen Möglichkeiten...darin wird er als der Christus erkannt...wir sehen in ihm Gottes Treue wirklich in der Tiefe der Hölle, *Römerbrief,* pp. 78-79.

# God's business card?

*No man knoweth who the Son is, but the Father; and who the Father is but the Son, and he to whom the Son will reveal him.*
**Luke 10:22**

BEAUCHIEF ABBEY
TRINITY SUNDAY
7TH JUNE 2009

Many people in industry, business, commerce and academia have business cards. No doubt some of you here in the Abbey today have, or have had, business cards. The reason for them is so that you can tell other people who you are, what your qualifications and business are, and how you can be contacted. They contain your name, your qualifications, what you have to offer, and your address, telephone and e-mail. I want to suggest this morning that one way of thinking about the Trinity is seeing it as God's business card – something there, not in order to give preachers nightmares once a year about how they are going to deal with abstruse theology, but because God wants us to know who he is, what his qualifications are, what he is about and how he can become known to us, and we to him.

The first item on a business card is a name, and we tend to forget that God has a special name, which comes over six thousand times in the Old Testament. We tend to overlook this because the Jews came to regard this name as so sacred that they ceased to pronounce it. Every time they came to it in the Bible – and this is what I do myself when reading the Old Testament in Hebrew – they read not the special name, which we think was pronounced something like *Yahveh*, but they read the word *adonai*, meaning 'Lord'. When the Bible was translated into Greek and Latin, and later into English, this tradition was maintained. The special name was given as 'Lord'; but you can recognise it by the way it is printed in English Bibles – with a capital 'L' and 'ord' in small capitals, thus, LORD, as opposed to Lord. However, the important thing is what the name meant. We are used in English to names derived from the crafts people once practised. The names Tanner, Cooper, Smith, Weaver, Thatcher, Fisher, Wright, all derive from crafts. God's special name in the Old Testament was connected with his deliverance of the Israelites from slavery in Egypt. When God appeared to Moses in the burning bush and commissioned him to lead the Israelites out of slavery, Moses asked, in effect, who are you? What is your name? (Exodus 3). What am I to tell the Israelites when they ask me who sent me? God's reply was 'I AM WHO I AM. Tell them that I AM has sent you'. In compiling God's business card we can put as his name I AM, plus, in brackets, (the one who liberates and sets free). The fact that God has a special name is important, because the word 'God' is not, strictly speaking, a name but the description of an object, a supreme being. A name establishes a relationship. When we give names to our pets they cease to be objects, such as 'cat' or 'dog'. The name we give them is part of our relationship with them. When people talk about God they are not usually talking about someone with whom they have some kind of relationship. As one writer has put it, God does not have an existence, he has a name.[45]

The second item is God's qualifications. There is much about these in the Old Testament that I could mention this morning, but I shall confine myself to a story about a house fire in which all the members of a family perished except for a child. Before the fire brigade arrived, a child's face was seen at a window, and a man from the crowd rushed forward, climbed up a hot metal drainpipe, got to the window, opened it and brought the child to safety. Having done this he gave the child into the care of a bystander, and promptly disappeared. The child not only lost its family, but had no members of a wider family

[45] Ton Veerkamp, Die Vernichtung des Baal. Auslegung der Königsbücher (1.17-2.11), Stuttgart: Alektor Verlag, 1983, p. 44.

who could support it. It was therefore put up for adoption. A man presented himself to the adoption agency and asked to adopt the child. When asked for his qualifications to do so, he showed them his hands. They were burnt and disfigured from when he had climbed the red hot drainpipe to rescue the child.[46] If we look at the hands and wrists of Jesus Christ we see the imprint of the nails that fastened him to the cross. They are among God's qualifications as the one who comes to set people free. So, on God's business card, we would have to put a cross to indicate his qualifications to carry on his business.

The third part of what I have to say may sound corny, but it is consonant with my point about the Trinity being concerned with God letting us know who he is and how we can be known by him. In the place where we would normally put our address, telephone and e-mail there would be a dove, the symbol of God's Spirit through whom he is active in the world. Within the outline of the dove we might also want to put other symbols, such as an open book to represent the Bible, God's word, or symbols of bread and wine, representing the visible and acted words of God's mercy extended to us in our Holy Communion.

The reason why there is a doctrine of the Trinity is because God wishes to make known who he is, what his purposes are, how he is qualified to carry them out, and how he can be known to us. It is not a piece of abstruse speculation. It is fundamental to the liberation and salvation that God wishes to give to us, and through us, to others. It is his business card.

---

[46] I heard this story from an Air Force chaplain in St. George's Church, Habbaniyah, Iraq in 1955. I do not know its source otherwise.

# The Prodigal Son

*This thy brother was dead, and is alive again; and was lost, and is found.*
**Luke 15:32**

BEAUCHIEF ABBEY
THIRD SUNDAY AFTER TRINITY
28TH JUNE 2009

The Parable of the Prodigal Son is one of the glories of the New Testament, and one that can have a profound effect upon those who hear it. In *The Times* obituary of Bishop Maurice Harland (who died on 29 September 1986 and who ordained me in 1964) it is recorded that he once had to minister to a man who was awaiting execution for a particularly nasty murder. He was locked into the cell with the man, who was smoking, sitting with his feet on the table, and smiling in a supercilious way. Harland read the Parable of the Prodigal Son, and its effect on the convicted man was such that he broke down in tears, was moved with remorse for what he had done and, before he went to his death, had been confirmed and had received Communion.

But there is another side. In my early Durham days I gave some talks in the parish of Pallion, near Sunderland, including one on this parable. It deeply offended one of the hearers. She had sacrificed either career or marriage in order to care for an elderly parent, and felt great offence at the treatment of the Elder Brother in the parable. It seemed to her that the parable was a charter for members of families who avoid their responsibilities, and who leave it to other siblings to look after elderly members of the family while they use their freedom to pursue their careers or their marriages. It is not difficult to feel sympathy for this point of view, and I have always been grateful to this woman for making me aware that it is easy to preach glib sermons about the Elder Brother without realising the hurt that this may cause to the many people who have sacrificed career or marriage or both, in order to care for members of their family. Let me say categorically that the parable is not intended to teach that those who avoid responsibilities will end up in a better position in the Kingdom of God than those who take their responsibilities seriously.

I want to approach the parable by thinking about the nature of forgiveness. We often hear people say, 'I shall forgive, but I won't forget', and this is often taken as a misunderstanding of what forgiveness is about. But forgiveness is not about forgetting. Indeed, it would be immoral to forget the great injustices that have occurred in recent years, and although our political leaders like to talk about 'drawing a line under things' or 'moving on' this is not the way that we should behave. Forgiveness is not about forgetting; it is about remembering in a creative way - remembering so that the past ceases to poison the present and the future, and ceases to cast a black shadow over all that we do. This is exemplified in the parable, and is the difference between the Father and the Elder Brother.

When the Prodigal returns he is a pathetic figure: malnourished, unshaven, dirty and clothed in rags. What he needs immediately is not to be reminded of the past he has wasted and ruined; he needs the opportunity to redeem the past by becoming the loyal son that he has previously failed to be. The Father uses the past creatively to make that possible. He remembers that the lad is his son, and treats him accordingly. The Prodigal is now in the best possible place to begin to put right what he had so disastrously done wrong. The Father's forgiveness is a creative use of the past in order to redeem the present and the future.

The attitude of the Elder Brother is different. For him, the past cannot be redeemed by the present and the future. If he, and not the Father, had been the one to see the Prodigal return, the outcome would have been different. We can imagine him saying something such as, 'Who do you think you are, coming back here in this pathetic state? You've had your chance and you've ruined it. Go and get help from your friends who helped you spend your money. You don't belong here!' In this case, the past would have triumphed over the present and the future, and would have succeeded in poisoning it and in casting its shadow over it. A human life would have been denied the chance to redeem the past.

This understanding of forgiveness has profound implications for us. The declaration of Absolution in our services is not a means of wiping clean a slate that has somehow been dirtied in the previous week or month. What we have done in the past is part of what we are in the present. It cannot be blotted out. What Absolution does is to declare that in God's sight, the past cannot hinder us from continuing as his sons and daughters, provided that we do not take his mercy for granted, as the Prodigal did not take his Father's mercy for granted. And it involves our willingness to serve God in the process of redeeming the past by using the present and the future in his service. The Gospel is not that God will accept us if we have spent a lifetime trying to redeem the past; the Gospel is that God accepts us as we are, so that in his service the past can be creatively transformed in the present and the future.

# *Hell*

*He cometh to judge the earth: he shall judge the world with righteousness, and the people with his truth.*
**Psalm 96:13**

BEAUCHIEF ABBEY
THIRD SUNDAY IN ADVENT
13TH DECEMBER 2009

The theme for the Third Sunday in Advent is traditionally that of hell, and that is what I want to talk about briefly this morning under three headings: first, the origin of the word "hell" and its New Testament background; secondly, the way it was interpreted, or rather misinterpreted in the Middle Ages and still is in some modern churches; and, thirdly, how the notion of hell can have positive meaning for Christians today.

The English word "hell" comes ultimately from a Nordic goddess of that similar name, who was the goddess of the underworld, the place of the departed; and so the word "hell" simply meant the place of the departed. But when it was used in the translations of the New Testament into English, it translated the Greek word *gehenna*, and *gehenna* or *gehinnom* was the name of a valley close to Jerusalem. In that valley rubbish was burned that could not be recycled and whose retention would have been a threat to the health of the community. There was a fire burning all the time there, and we have a hint of that in the reading from Mark 9, where it speaks about hell where the fire is always burning. I do not know whether anyone has done a PhD on recycling and rubbish disposal in Ancient Israel (there's a piece of work waiting to be done, I think, and I would be rather interested to read it; we have enough problems of our own in Sheffield, trying to deal with our recycling and our rubbish collections) but in the Ancient World the sort of materials that could not easily be disposed of, and which would have caused disease if they had been left around, were burned. In the case of Jerusalem this was in the valley of *gehinnom*. Although the aim, therefore, was to destroy what was burned, at the heart of it was a purification process – and that becomes important for what I have to say in a moment.

For other reasons this particular valley, the valley of *gehinnom,* also came to be associated with punishment and judgement at the end of the world. Now, in the earliest Church, some theologians took up the idea of purification: the point of hell was not so much to punish people as to purify people, to get rid of the impurities in their lives, so that what was left was the pure metal. One of the great exponents of this point of view was a man called Origen, a great biblical scholar, who according to tradition gave his life as a martyr for his Christian faith around the year 254 in the great persecutions of the Church under the Roman Emperor Decius. Origen was accused, wrongly of holding the view that even the devil could be redeemed and saved: that the purifying process could even get rid of all that was evil in the devil and, in the devil's case, find something worth preserving. Origen denied believing this, but the mud stuck, and in the sixth and seventh centuries there were Councils of the Church that condemned in particular the teaching of Origen, and also any idea that the purpose of hell was to get rid of the rubbish and discover the pure metal, so that there would be something worth redeeming in as many people as possible.

And so we pass, secondly, to the medieval idea of hell and its modern misunderstanding in some churches today, as a place of eternal torment and punishment. Now, I think that idea was a grave mistake, because it turned what ought to be good news into bad news; it turned a promise into a threat. Think of it this way: let us imagine two families. Both outwardly appear to be unified, and yet in one of the families the basis for unity is fear. The head of the house, the man, if he chooses, can use such physical force or mental abuse towards his wife and his children that they are terrified to trouble him in any way, lest they be punished; and so, in that way, based upon fear, the unity of that family is maintained. Contrast with that another family, where the basis of its unity is mutual respect and love and trust. I am sure we would all say the second family is the one that we would most admire. And yet the medieval idea of hell and its modern adherents is asking us to endorse the first model, a model in which it is fear, not respect or love, that governs the loyalty of those who are within the household of faith. Let us think of our own reasons for following, in our own halting and inadequate ways, the path of Christ. We do not do it because of fear; we do it because we have in various different ways caught sight of some vision, something that we wish not only to possess, but that we wish to possess us. It is a little like the parable Jesus told of the Pearl of Great Price. There is a merchant dealing with costly pearls, and suddenly he comes across one that is of such immense worth in his eyes that he wants to sell all his other pearls in order to gain this one. Similarly, in the Bible, or in our worship, in the teaching of Jesus, or in some other way, we have caught a vision of something to which we wish our lives to be indexed; and in different ways we have made sacrifices in order that we might possess or, more importantly, that we might be possessed by this vision, so that as Christians we have good news to proclaim: not a gospel of fear, but a gospel in which we seek to share with others that vision which has captured our imaginations and around which we have sought, however unworthily and inadequately, to fashion our lives.

And now the third point. What positive things can we say about the doctrine of hell? The first thing is it assures us that in this world it matters whether we are like Adolf Hitler or whether we are like Mother Teresa. I would hate to live in a world where it did not matter whether you were Adolf Hitler, Pol Pot or the Yorkshire Ripper, on the one hand, or Mother

Teresa of Calcutta, Florence Nightingale or the great Quaker reformer of prisons in the early nineteenth century, Elizabeth Fry, on the other. The doctrine of hell assures us that there is, at the heart of things, a justice that will be worked out. That should give us some cause for satisfaction, but it can give us no cause for *self*-satisfaction. We might want to say that we are glad that those perpetrators of evil will get their come-uppance, but we cannot do that with any sense of certainty on our own part. We, as much as they, are dependent upon the mercy of God. The judgement, and that is the good news, is judgement of ourselves, as we are made better persons to be fit for the better world that God wants to bring about. The Old Testament has some harsh words about people who think judgement is all right for everybody else except for them. There were Israelites in Old Testament times who thought the Day of the Lord would bring judgement upon Israel's neigh-bours, but not upon Israel. Amos says in his trenchant way:

> Woe unto you that desire the day of the LORD! ... [The day of the LORD] is darkness, and not light; as if a man did flee from a lion, and a bear met him [47]

And so judgement for all of us is part of the Good News, and I love the conclusion to Psalm 96, which reads as follows:

> Let the heavens be glad, and let the earth rejoice; let the sea make a noise and all that therein is. Let the field be joyful and all that is in it. Then shall all the trees of the wood rejoice before the LORD, for he cometh, for he cometh to judge the earth and with righteousness to judge the world and the people with his truth [48]

---

[47] Amos 5:18-20

[48] Psalm 96:11-13

That is a very modern text - the field that we can devastate and exploit so that it becomes a desert; the sea that we pollute; the trees of the wood which we chop down – all these things can rejoice that God is going to come to judge the earth with his righteousness and with his truth.

So, granted that, how is it all going to work? Here there are many things that I do not know, and I can only simply raise some questions; but I do so around a passage that will be very familiar to us, taken from Philippians 2, and it is possibly a very ancient Christian hymn which is being quoted here by St Paul. Remember how it goes? He speaks about Christ

> who, being in the form of God, thought it not robbery to be equal with God, but made himself of no reputation, and took upon him the form of a servant and was made in the likeness of men. [49]

And he goes on to say that –

> God also hath highly exalted him, and given him a name that is above every name, that at the name of Jesus *every* knee should bow... and that *every* tongue should confess that Jesus Christ is Lord, to the glory of God the Father[50]

Does it mean *every* tongue? Does it mean Adolf Hitler and Pol Pot and the Yorkshire Ripper? I don't know. And how is it to be brought about? Are the fires traditionally associated with hell the fires of shame and remorse? Well, perhaps. Perhaps already in the lives of people such as Mother Teresa, Florence Nightingale and Elizabeth Fry we see the same sacrificial self-

---

[49] Philippians 2:6-7

[50] Philippians 2:9-11

giving love that can move us to shame and move us to wish for better things. Because one thing is clear: it seems to me that however this process is to come about – that every knee and every tongue will acknowledge the Lordship of Jesus Christ – it does not come about through the power of the bully, the power of the dictator, the person who has the power to torture and terrify us until our wills are broken to do what is desired. What is being spoken about is the force of sacrificial self-giving love on the part of others. How far will it work? I do not know. At the end of the day, will there be those who because they cannot, or will not, exist in a sphere in which God is all in all, wish simply to have their existence completely terminated?

I recently came across a remarkable definition of eternal damnation in a biography of Sophie Scholl. Sophie, together with her brother Hans and a friend Christoph Probst, were part of a resistance group called the White Rose at the University of Munich in the 1940s. Deeply committed Catholics, they circulated leaflets to their fellow students calling upon them to oppose the Nazi regime. They were detected, arrested, and executed by guillotine on 22 February 1943. Sophie was aged 21. The year before her death she came across a definition of eternal damnation as the condition in which it was no longer possible to love anyone, and she wondered, in a letter to a friend, whether it also included the condition in which it was no longer possible to be loved.[51]

---

[51] Barbara Beuys, *Sophie Scholl. Biografie* (Darmstadt: Wissenschaftliche Buchgesellschaft, 2010, p. 377). This paragraph was not in the sermon as originally preached, but added later.

That leads me to my final word, because as I think about hell and all that it implies, I think about a passage that comes at the end of the Book of Revelation:

> And I saw a new heaven and a new earth; for the first heaven and the first earth were passed away... and I heard a great voice out of heaven saying, "Behold, the tabernacle of God is with men; and he will dwell with them and they shall be his people and God himself shall be with them and be their God; and God shall wipe away all tears from their eyes, and there shall be no more death, neither sorrow, nor crying, neither shall there be any more pain, for the former things are passed away." And he that sat upon the throne said, "Behold, I make all things *new*." [52]

---

[52] Revelation 21:1,3-5

# The Temptations

*Jesus was led by the Spirit into the wilderness, being forty days tempted by the devil*
**Luke 4:1**

BEAUCHIEF ABBEY
FIRST SUNDAY IN LENT
21ST FEBRUARY 2010

I want to try a thought experiment this morning. Instead of thinking about the Gospel that I have just read as an encounter between Jesus and Satan, I want us to think of it as an encounter between ourselves and Satan in relation to our belief in God. There is a very simple reason for this: it is possible to preach very fine and helpful sermons (and perhaps I have done this myself on more than one occasion) without thinking of the *significance* of the encounter between Jesus and the devil two thousand years ago. We can be quite pleased that Jesus, contemplating the shape and strategy of his mission, should have decided not to do the things the devil tempted him to do. And that, I say, can be very fine and helpful; and yet it leaves it all locked in the past, two thousand years ago. We can come away with a feeling, "Isn't it good that Jesus defeated the devil?" But I want to ask the question, "Has, in fact, the devil defeated us?"

Let us start with the second of the temptations, the temptation of Jesus to cast himself down from the Temple, because if he did so (the devil says) God would intervene and save him. Now, I don't know about you, but I get rather tired of hearing the clever interviewers, not only on the Radio 4 *Today* programme, but sometimes on the *Sunday* programme, who ask the following questions of people, especially if they are Christians and they have some tragedy in their life: "Why do you think God has let this happen to you? Has this not destroyed your faith in God? Don't you think that God should have intervened? Where was God in the tsunami that struck the part of the world that it did a couple of Christmases ago?" And they also ask this sort of question, "Why go on believing in God when these things happen to you?" Are those questions any different from the one that was put by the devil to Jesus, "Cast yourself down, for if you do, God will intervene"?

Now, thinking about the first of the temptations, when the devil suggests that Jesus should turn stones into bread, perhaps we can feel a little bit more confident. Gone are the days when we felt that it was entirely up to God to make sure that the injustices of the world that we contrive should be put right. It is good there are such things as consciousness about fair trade and that Christian Aid should be so prominent and do such good work. In the year 2000, the Jubilee Campaign was very successful in drawing the attention of the rulers of the world to the debt problem in the Third World countries, and the fact that we should do something about it. These things have been little triumphs – and yet of course as we see at the moment, alas, in the financial crash and banking crisis facing us that the leaders of the rich world are capable of bailing out the banks, but apparently not able still, or yet, to do anything about Third World debt, which is trifling in comparison with the sums of money that are suddenly being found to prop up the banks. So although perhaps we are not entirely bad on this territory, there is perhaps something to worry us.

But when we come to the third temptation I am especially worried. The devil says to Jesus, "If you bow down and worship me, all these riches of the kingdoms of the world will be yours." Now, it can be argued that it was a bad day for the Church when, early in the fourth century, the Roman Emperor Constantine decided to become a Christian and Christianity became the official religion of the Roman Empire, because undoubtedly the Church, if it had not done so before, now took on all the trappings of a great world organisation with the wealth, the power, the hierarchy, and everything else that involved. Now, of course there were other voices in the Church. The monastic movement - for all that it had the weakness of depending for its existence on the world that it shunned - at least the monastic movement was an attempt to say, "No, look, there must be an alternative". We here at the Abbey must be very proud of the fact that, whatever may have been the motives of the people who built the Abbey, at least the people who worked here, did not do so in order to make a profit for themselves. They did so, in order to go out; to take comfort and healing and hope to the people in the surrounding area. It was therefore an exercise in something that was not a commitment to the rule and the ideology of the kingdoms of this world.

It is interesting that so far, for most of its history, the Church believed and taught that it was wrong to charge interest on loans. Until the time of the Reformation, the Church believed that the Bible and Jesus had forbidden the charging of interest on loans. At the Reformation Luther, to his credit, upheld the ancient Christian traditions of the Church. It was Calvin who swept aside the arguments that had been used up to that time against the charging of interest, and who played a part in enabling capitalism as we know it to develop. One of the ironies of today's situation is that what was rightly or wrongly believed by the Church for most of its history to be the teaching of the Bible and the teaching of Jesus, is upheld today by the Islamic community and Islamic banking, because within Islamic banking the charging of interest is forbidden, as in the Qur'àn. Islamic banking does not go along the lines of what has brought us to the current dire situation – the whole business, not just of charging interest, but of lending people money they cannot afford to pay back. So, this is a very fascinating question. Is it the case that in our post-Christian world we have allowed ourselves to be tempted by what the devil offered Jesus - to serve the kingdoms of the world with all their wealth and glory? Is it the case that we have succumbed to that?

Now, these are challenging thoughts, and this is one of the things that Lent is about. What it does boil down to, if we take these things together, is that the devil may not have defeated Jesus, but he seems to have defeated us. The upshot is this: what the devil wants us to do, if we are going to have a God at all, is for us to have a God who is our creation; a God who does not intervene in our world for most of the time, but lets us get on with running or ruining the world; a God who is only there to intervene when things get rather bad - when we have massacres or holocausts; a God who has to conform to our notions of what it means for him to exist; a God who should be there for our interests, for our concerns, almost to the point that if God does not conform to our standards, then we are not going to bother with him at all. That is the upshot of all this, if the devil has persuaded us to succumb to those temptations to which Jesus did not succumb; because, ulti-mately, that sort of God is no God at all. That sort of God is only our creation, and because it is our creation, it has no more power to help us than we have power to help ourselves, and when we look at the record of the human race, it is hardly an impressive one.

So, on this First Sunday in Lent, this leaves us with a chal-lenge: What sort of God do we want? What sort of God do we believe in? Is it the God of our own creation, the God that the devil has tempted us to accept? Or is it the God and Father of our Lord Jesus Christ, King of the King of Kings, the Holy

One, blessed be he, who goes against all our hopes and expectations, thank goodness, because only therein lies our hope; who sent his Son to die and rise for us? Is that the God we believe in? Let us hope and pray that the God of all mercies will take us to himself, inspire us as a congregation, and lead us out in our mission, as we seek to be witnesses for him.

# Bibliography

*New Every Morning*, London: The British Broadcasting Corporation, 1936.

*Rejoice and Sing*, Oxford: Oxford University Press, 1991.

**K. Barth**, *The Epistle to the Romans* (translated by E. C. Hoskins), Oxford: Oxford University Press, 1968.

**Z. Bauman**, *Liquid Life*, Cambridge: Polity Press, 2005

**Barbara Beuys**, *Sophie Scholl. Biografie*, Darmstadt: Wissenschaftliche Buchgesellschaft, 2010.

**R.E. Brown**, *The Gospel according to John* (Anchor Bible), London: Geoffrey Chapman, 1971.

**G. D'Oyly and R. Mant**, *Notes Explanatory and Practical to the Authorised Version of the Holy Bible*, London: SPCK, 1848.

**M. Green, D. Holloway, D. Watson**, *The Church and Homosexuality. A Positive Answer to the Current Debate*, London: Hodder and Stoughton, 1980.

**J. Jeremias**, *Jerusalem zur Zeit Jesu*, Göttingen: Vandenhoeck & Ruprecht, 1958.

**W.R. Matthews, et al.**, *William Temple: An Estimation & an Appreciation*, London: James Clark & Co., 1946.

**W.G. Peck**, 'William Temple as Social Thinker' in W.R. Matthews, et al., *William Temple: An Estimation & an Appreciation*, London: James Clark & Co., 1946.

**Nancy le Plastrier Warner**, *Hugh Compton Warner: The story of a vocation*, London: SPCK, 1958.

**P. Radin**, *Primitive Man as Philosopher*, New York: Dover Publications, 1957.

**J. Ratzinger**, 'Ascension of Christ' in K. Rahner (ed.), *Encyclopedia of Theology. A Concise Sacramentum Mundi*, London: Burns & Oates, 1975

**K. Rahner** (ed.), *Encyclopedia of Theology. A Concise Sacramentum Mundi*, London: Burns & Oates, 1975

**J.W. Rogerson**, *Nine O'Clock Service and Other Sermons*, Sheffield: Urban Theology Unit, 2002.

**H.R.L. Sheppard**, *Two Days Before. Simple Thoughts about our Lord on the Cross*, London: SCM Press, 1924.

**A. Smitmans**, *Das Wunder von Kana. Die Auslegung von Joh, 1-11 bei den Vätern und heute*, Tübingen, 1966.

**J. Stevenson,** *A New Eusebius. Documents illustrative of the history of the Church to A.D. 337*, London: SPCK, 1957.

**Ton Veerkamp**, *Die Vernichtung des Baal. Auslegung der Königsbücher (1.17-2.11)*, Stuttgart: Alektor Verlag, 1983

# Index of Biblical References

# Index of Persons & Subjects

# The Preacher

# J. W. Rogerson

John William Rogerson was born in London in 1935 and educated at Bec School, Tooting, the Joint Services School for Linguists, Coulsdon Common, where he completed an intensive course in Russian, and the Universities of Manchester, Oxford and Jerusalem, where he studied theology and Semitic languages. He was ordained in 1964 and served as Assistant Curate at St. Oswald's, Durham. From 1964 to 1975 he was Lecturer, and from 1975 to 1979 Senior Lecturer in Theology at Durham University before moving in 1979 to become Professor and Head of the Department of Biblical Studies at the University of Sheffield, retiring in 1996. He was made an honorary Canon of Sheffield Cathedral in 1982 and an Emeritus Canon in 1995. In addition to many essays and scholarly articles, his published books include *Myth in Old Testament Interpretation* (1974), *Psalms* (Cambridge Bible Commentary, with J.W. McKay, 1977), *Anthropology and the Old Testament* (1978), *Old Testament Criticism in the Nineteenth Century: England and Germany* (1984), *The New Atlas of the Bible* (1985, translated into nine languages), *W. M. L . de Wette., Founder of Modern Biblical Criticism. An Intellectual Biography* (1991), *The Bible and Criticism in Victorian Britain. Profiles of F. D. Maurice and William Robertson Smith* (1995), *An Introduction to the Bible* (1999, 3rd edition 2012), *Theory and Practice in Old Testament Ethics* (2004), *According to the Scriptures? The Challenge of using the Bible in Social, Moral and Political Questions* (2007), *A Theology of the Old Testament. Cultural memory, communication and being human* (2009), *The Art of Biblical Prayer* (2011). He was awarded the degree of Doctor of Divinity for published work by the University of Manchester in 1975, and has also been awarded the Honorary Degree of Doctor of Divinity by the University of Aberdeen and the Honorary Degree of Dr. theol. by the Friedrich-Schiller-Universität, Jena and the Albert-Ludwigs-Universität, Freiburg im Breisgau.